THE TURNING POINT

FOSTERING THROUGH THE EYES OF A CHILD — VOLUME 3

THE TURNING POINT

THE JOY OF BECOMING A PERSON

DESMOND TOMLINSON

MANGIFERA
BLOOM
Port St Lucie

Copyright © 2020 Desmond Tomlinson
All rights reserved.

Published by Mangifera Bloom, Port St Lucie

All rights reserved. No part of this book may be reproduced, stored, or transmitted by any means—whether auditory, graphic, mechanical, or electronic—without written permission of the publisher except in the case of brief excerpts used in critical articles and reviews.
Please send inquiries to mangiferabloom@gmail.com.

Find out more at https://www.fosteringthroughtheeyesofachild.net

1st Edition

ISBN: 978-1-7342500-2-2 (Paperback)
ISBN: 978-1-7342500-6-0 (ebook)

Library of Congress Control Number: 2020909304

Edited by Mikel Benton
Cover illustration by Michael Rohani
Book design by DesignForBooks.com

Printed in the U.S.A.

CONTENTS

THE EXORDIUM IX

  Dedication ix
  How My Autobiography Is Organized xi
  Conventions Used xiii
  Additional Content xiv

ACKNOWLEDGMENT AND OVERVIEW XV

  Ms. Clemmie xv
  Fredricka Lucy Brady (Aunt Lucy) xvi
  Mrs. Laurel HoSang (HEART Mom) xvii
  Mr. Leroy Tyson (Sir T) xvii
  My Fellow Jamaicans xviii
  Family Overview xix

CHAPTER 1 A DAY OF RECKONING 1

CHAPTER 2 TRANSITION 17

  Home at Last 19
  The Value of Work 30
  The Connection 32
  In Search of a Foster Parent 35
  Lost Opportunity 39

Contents

CHAPTER 3 THE ALPHA (α) 47

The Unforgettable Journey   47
Finally, Home   49
Compare and Contrast Foster Parents   52
Rebuilding the Foundation of Life   62
Finally, Back in School   75
The Unexpected Appearance   83
In Search of Higher Education   89
Financial Hiccup   96
The Financial Breakthrough   99
The First Harvest   107

CHAPTER 4 REUNITED WITH MY BIOLOGICAL FAMILY 111

The Search Engines That Never Quit   113
Miraculous Reunification   115
Meeting My Eldest Sibling for the First Time   117
Off to Visit My Mother and Siblings   119
The Much-anticipated Reunion   121

CHAPTER 5 WHAT'S NEXT 127

Crossing the Finish Line   127
Life after Albert Town Secondary School   128
Let's Wait a Little While Longer   135

CHAPTER 6 KNOWLEDGE FROM THE HEART 143

No More Delay, Let the Training Begin   152
Faith Based Journey   156
Reuniting with my Former Foster Parents Adopted Daughter   158

Academic Turbulence   159
The Unexplainable Intervention   160
Meeting My HEART Family   162
Academy Perks   164
The Final Leg of the Journey   164
Celebration Day   166
Life After Graduating   170
Receiving Our Marching Orders   171

CHAPTER 7 LIFE WITH MY EXTENDED FAMILY   173

Off to My First Fulltime Job   175

CHAPTER 8 MY FIRST ENDEAVOR   179

Hurricane Gilbert (Wild Gilbert)   180
Opportunity Comes Knocking   187

CHAPTER 9 CAREER ADVANCEMENT   189

My Wishful Job Prospect   190
Off to My Long-anticipated Interview   192

CHAPTER 10 LIFE IN THE CITY OF MONTEGO BAY   205

My Wish Come True   205
Academic Outlook   214
Jump Start My Academic Career   216
Genuine Personality Traits   217
The Mysterious Reunification   221
Opportunity Comes Knocking   226
The Miraculous Breakthrough   232
Meeting My Trusted Mediator   233
The Risky Endeavor   234

The Daredevil Driva   238
The Joy and Disappointment Associated with
the US Embassy Visa Process   241
The Final Countdown   245

JAMAICA – THE JOURNEY   250

APPENDIX A THE UNEXPLAINABLE INTERVENTION   251

APPENDIX B GENEROSITY ABOUNDS   255

REFERENCES   257

THE EXORDIUM

Dedication

First and foremost, I would like to give God the glory for bestowing unto me health, strength, happiness, and the many other wonderful blessings of life. Second, I would like to take this opportunity to pay one final tribute by dedicating this volume to the memories of my loving and compassionate foster mother, Fredricka Lucy Brady (Aunt Lucy), who has made all the difference in my life.

I would like to commence by highlighting two of the more pressing questions that I keep pondering over since the day I decided to share my life story. The first is, what defining message will my life experiences convey to humanity as a whole? And second, will humanity be receptive to such a message? At first, I thought I had these questions all figured out, but the more I think about them, the more I realize that I may never be able to come up with definitive answers. However, in my quest to uncover the answers, I would hope that you join me as I traverse the emotional, at times the roller-coaster-like, journey of my life. At first, I thought about the possibility of conveying my story verbally. On second thought, I realized that this method would certainly not be the most effective. With that in mind, I set out to tell my story in a written form and hope to accomplish the following:

The Exordium

- To highlight the wonderful blessings of God that have transformed my life
- To express the overwhelming and unyielding compassion that was bestowed unto me by my foster mother, Fredricka Lucy Brady (Aunt Lucy)
- To establish the fact that life is not just about my inner circle or me, but also about individuals who have not been fortunate to be loved and cared for, especially throughout their early childhood and adolescent years
- To acknowledge and credit the many individuals and institutions that have provided me with the help and support I desperately needed throughout my early childhood years.
- To highlight the fact that the desire to pray and the need to persevere are the two most important characteristics that I relied on each day to overcome life's obstacles[1]
- To never give up when you find yourself going through life darkest moments because I believe that God is always there with you
- To shine a light on the foster care system and stress the need for us to develop and implement policies to protect children and the less fortunate

---

[1] Although I have intentionally left out tangible aspects such as financial needs, it does not mean that I do not value their importance. However, the point I am conveying is this: financial and other material possessions are not characteristics of one's being. I have highlighted this concept in detail, especially throughout the compare-and-contrast sections dealing with my current and former foster parents.

The Exordium

- To share the experiences that have allowed me to realize the true meaning of fostering. Also, to share the stark differences between my current (Aunt Lucy) and my former foster parents' actions and how they apply to us today.[2]
- To provide inspiration and comfort to all, particularly the less fortunate (orphans) who have gone through or find themselves going through challenging times

How My Autobiography Is Organized

My autobiography is presented in four volumes. The first three volumes cover the unpredictable, life-changing events that occurred while I was living on the tropical island of Jamaica. The fourth reflects the transformational journey of my life after I migrated to the United States of America.

Volume 1, *The Separation* – this volume takes into account the following:

- Life with my father
- The emotional separation when my brother and I were forcefully removed from our father's care and transferred to an orphanage

---

[2] The most obvious are the actions taken by two foster parents. One individual (Aunt Lucy) who promoted the well-being of others, including the less fortunate children. While the other who disregarded and, at times, degraded the well-being of others, including the less fortunate children. This is why I have used this experience to challenge our hearts to pursue justice and peace above self-acclaimed interests.

- The joyous reunification when my brother and I were transferred from the orphanage back to our father's care
- The emotional separation when my brother, my sisters, and I were forcefully removed from our father's care and divvied up between orphanages
- The transfer of my brother and me from the orphanage to our mother's care
- The emotional separation when my brother and I were forcefully removed from our mother's care and returned to the orphanage

Volume 2, *Woka Man* – this volume takes into account the following:

- The transfer of my brother and me from the orphanage to a foster home
- The eternal, physical, and emotional separation that occurred when my brother was transferred to a correctional institution
- The remaining time I spent with my first foster parents including how and why I was also removed from their care

Volume 3, *The Turning Point* – this volume takes into account the following:

- Transition to and from a temporary foster home
- When and how I was united with my wonderful, caring, loving foster mother, Aunt Lucy

- Reunion with my biological family, including my only brother
- The continuation of my academic, professional, social, and *spiritual* journey

Volume 4, *A Dream Come True* – this volume takes into account the following:

- The remaining precious and unforgettable time I spent with my wonderful, caring, loving foster mother, Aunt Lucy
- The journey to a land far, far away to fulfill my academic dream
- The unimaginable but inspiring and transformative academic, professional, social, and *spiritual* opportunities that continue to shape and reshape my life
- The miraculous birth of life and the family of a lifetime

Conventions Used

To maintain the originality of individual quotes, phrases, and humor, I have incorporated the Jamaican Patois (Patwa) along with the English translations. However, in some cases, I have paraphrased both the Jamaican Patois and English translations as a way to maintain contextuality. Please bear in mind that the Jamaican Patois does not have a definitive structure. Therefore, the spelling and pronunciation of certain words could differ slightly. There are many sources and variations; however, I have relied on the *Jabari Authentic Jamaican Dictionary of the Jamic Language* as a guide (Reynolds 2006).

Although this book is my autobiography, I have taken the initiative to highlight the many acts of kindness bestowed unto me by family members, friends, acquaintances, strangers, and prominent institutions. These individuals and institutions are the many parts that have made my life whole. They have provided me with life's essentials and more. I have also been blessed to have received a lifetime of spiritual and moral support that has guided my actions and the way I perceived my fellow humankind.

Finally, I do hope that you will enjoy a smile and a little laughter as you read my tidbits of humor. I must also warn you that a number of my witticisms might go, swoosh, right over your head because they might be technologically funneled or skewed to a particular culture or era; or in the words of a teenager, they might come across as lame or botched. For the humor that you do not have a clue about, you are just going to have to wave the Google magic wand for further clarification.

Additional Content

To complement my written autobiography, I have created the www.fosteringthroughtheeyesofachild.net website to provide additional information and content, such as pictures and links for the subjects and topics that have been referenced throughout the different volumes. Also, the reader or interested party is more than welcome to use this website to provide an ongoing discussion regarding the content of my autobiography and other topics associated with the development and well-being of children.

ACKNOWLEDGMENT AND OVERVIEW

Please bear with me while I take this opportunity to introduce, and in some instances, express my sincere thanks and gratitude to several individuals, including family members and friends, whom I have mentioned throughout this volume of my autobiography.

Ms. Clemmie

I would also like to say a special thank you to Ms. Clemmie. I remember the day my former foster parents dropped me off at the CDA office and left me with nowhere to go or no one to turn to for support. Throughout those crucial moments, Ms. Clemmie reached out to me and invited me into her home and into her life. She did not have much, but that did not stop her from taking on the responsibility of caring for me. Although I spent only a short time (one month and eight days, to be precise) with her, I will always cherish the precious moments we shared.

Acknowledgment and Overview

Fredricka Lucy Brady (Aunt Lucy)

I want to use every fiber of my inner being to say a special thank you to my foster mother, Ms. Fredricka "Lucy" Brady or Aunt Lucy, as everyone in the community affectionately knew her. There are not enough words in the universe that could ever quantify or express her compassion and her love.

The foster mother of a lifetime, Fredricka Lucy Brady (Aunt Lucy).

Although she is no longer with me physically, she has left me with a lifetime of memories that I will always cherish. Aunt Lucy poured out her love and kindness unto me, just as any loving and caring mother would bestow unto her child. The magnitude of her unyielding compassion was even more revealing when I had a chance to compile my autobiography. This is why I can say, unequivocally, without a shred of doubt, that Fredricka "Lucy" Brady gave me a second chance for life and the pursuit of happiness. Without her perseverance and her relentless determination, I would not have been reunited with my biological parents and siblings. She gave me the courage and determination to persevere against all the odds. Her love and compassion opened my eyes and my understanding to realize the true meaning of fostering.

Acknowledgment and Overview

Mrs. Laurel HoSang (HEART Mom)

I would like to introduce yet another mom, Mrs. Laurel HoSang. I also refer to her as my HEART mom, the reasons for which will become apparent shortly. Mrs. HoSang has been a mother to me ever since the first day I came to know her, which is some twenty-nine years ago. She has treated me like a son. Mrs. HoSang opened her doors and welcomed me into her home and her life. Her moral and compassionate support has made an unforgettable impact on my life.

My HEART mom (Laurel HoSang)

Mr. Leroy Tyson (Sir T)

I would like to take this moment to recognize Mr. Leroy Tyson (Sir T), yet another influential person who has played a significant role in my life. Mr. Tyson provided me with the support and guidance I needed throughout a crucial juncture of my life. He assisted me with my academic studies and became my lifelong mentor. If you happened to be around Mr. Tyson, he would be the first to render his time and even financial support to make sure you understood the importance of education. Mr. Tyson has been mentoring kids for several decades, especially those from his home parish of Westmoreland. Not only is he a preacher in this regard, but he is also a person who embodies the "practice what you preach" philosophy. Mr. Tyson is a big believer in knowledge acquisition, and has spent a tremendous amount of his time, effort, and money toward his academic advancement. He is a true humanitarian, and I do believe that he deserves more than a Nobel Peace Prize for his significant contributions to promoting the lives of many young Jamaicans.

My Fellow Jamaicans

I would like to extend my sincere thanks and deepest gratitude to the members of the Child Development Agency (CDA) of Jamaica. This dedicated group of individuals has worked tirelessly on my behalf from the very day (August 13, 1975) I was assigned to their care through to the day (August 13, 1987) I received my honorable discharge from the foster care system.

I would like to say a special thank you to my two favorite CDA officers, Ms. Davis and Mrs. Stewart. If it were not for their keen foresight and swift actions, I would most likely have been transferred to Copse (juvenile Place of Safety/Correctional Institution for boys) instead of being placed into the care of a compassionate and loving foster mother, Aunt Lucy. They went above and beyond their call of duty to make my well-being their priority.

Finally, I would like to extend my sincere thanks and gratitude to all my fellow Jamaicans who have helped me to realize my dreams. Without your tax participation and other forms of charitable contributions, it would not have been possible for me to acquire life's essentials and more. Your moral and financial support is what kept me going. I am grateful that you have supported my academic dreams. I would like to remind you that when I was hungry, you gave me food; when I was thirsty, you gave me a drink; and when I was homeless, you provided a home for me.

Acknowledgment and Overview

Therefore, I can say with much sincerity, that your kindness and outstanding support have not and will not be forgotten.

Family Overview

I would like to elaborate briefly on my siblings Pauline, Paulette, Euphema, Grace, and George Tomlinson. This outline of the family structure will help to put references into context throughout the remainder of my autobiography. For a more in-depth overview of Pauline, Paulette, and George Tomlinson, please refer to volumes 1 and volume 2.

First, Euphema and Grace are my older sisters from my father's side of the family. Euphema (Inez) Tomlinson is the eldest of my four sisters. Although she was born into a poor family and had to raise two children, mostly on her own, she did not let those limitations hinder her progress. To make a better life for herself and the rest of the family, Inez migrated from Haddo, which is a small farming village in the parish of Westmoreland, to the city of Montego Bay, St. James. There, she started working as a bus conductress until she was able to own and operate her own business. Her philosophy is always to extend a helping hand to her siblings. She assumed the role of a mother to her siblings and total strangers, even if it meant giving up her comfort. If you get to know her, you will learn rather quickly that she is always happy and always greets others with a big and pleasant smile.

Grace (Gracie) Tomlinson, my second eldest sister on my father's side passed away, leaving her two young children to fend for themselves. This was the case because their fathers were not present in their lives. Gracie, from what I

Acknowledgment and Overview

From left to right, Euphema (Inez), Paulette, and Pauline Tomlinson.

heard and from the short time that I came to know her, was a very kind and loving person. If it were not for her relentless perseverance, I probably would not have known my correct date of birth. When I was experiencing difficulties obtaining my birth certificate, Gracie took matters into her own hands and went directly to the government office, personally searching through thousands of non-computerized records to locate mine. She allowed me to celebrate my first birthday at age twenty. Gracie never stopped searching until she found the orphanage where our sisters, Pauline and Paulette, were residing. She made the necessary arrangements and reunited them with the family.

Here is a picture of my only brother and me (from right to left, George and Desmond)

Acknowledgment and Overview

However, a dark chapter emerged when she became addicted to drugs. Her addiction sent her life into a downward spiral. Her drug addiction came as a shock to the entire family because everyone, including me, had the utmost respect for her judgment. From what I heard, Gracie was a very straightforward, no-nonsense type of person. Therefore, for her to have ventured down this dark and lonely road was very difficult for us to grasp. One thing I learned from this ordeal is the fact that no one, regardless of age, race, gender, or creed, is immune from peer pressure and bad influences.

Nevertheless, the pressing question that we need to ask ourselves is this: Do we have strong foundational values and principles to stand on whenever we find ourselves being tested in such a manner? Unfortunately, because of her actions, Gracie had lost sight of her children, her family, and her own life. Michael spent a lot of money on his mother's medical care, but, in the end, money was not enough to save her.

Gracie's willpower was not strong enough to overcome the addiction, and the family watched helplessly as she faded away from existence. Whenever I visited the family, I was always heartbroken because it was a painful sight to see what had become of my sister. Every time that I recall this incident, it reminds me of a Bible verse, "There is a way that seems right to a man, but its end is the way to death" (Proverbs 14:12, ESV). Although this experience was very unfortunate, I do hope that it reminds us, more so the younger generation, that we are not invincible and that we are susceptible to peer pressure. Therefore, my advice is that we listen to our internal voices rather than the voices of those who mean us harm.

CHAPTER 1

A DAY OF RECKONING

The day my foster parents drove me back to the Child Development Agency (CDA) was one of the loneliest times of my life. I felt as though the world was really closing in on me and I was standing all alone in the middle of nowhere. At that moment, the tears that were trickling down my cheeks started pouring down again. Little did I realize how attached I had become to my foster parents, even though I had been living in an environment in which I was constantly being abused. That day, it was quite difficult for me to grasp what was really happening. I just could not believe that my life was going through yet another traumatic and emotional transformation.

I remember the day when George and I had been taken from the orphanage and placed into the care of our foster parents. I truly believed that this would bring us stability and an end to our rollercoaster lives. I honestly believed that we had found a home and the parents of a lifetime! Little did I realize that I would find myself at a crucial point such as this. Little did I realize that life's rollercoaster was not yet through having its ups and downs with me.

Chapter 1

Before I proceed, I would like to stress the following point as it pertains to a person exercising due diligence before taking actions that will inevitably have enormous consequences on the lives of the innocent. On that day, I was very fortunate that Ms. Davis did not accept the false premise that my foster parents were using to justify their "righteous" indignation. Instead, she exercised due diligence and thoroughly examined the fabricated charges (theft, gambling, and seduction of the female children in the household) that my former foster parents had presented against me. Had she failed in such regard, then the outcome would have constituted a gross injustice, which is precisely where the Child Development Agency had fallen short with regard to my only brother and the other foster children. If the same thoughtful consideration and examination had been applied to my brother's case, then the agency would not have allowed him to be transferred to a juvenile correctional institution (Copse), thus contributing to his lifelong physical and psychological suffering. Therefore, it is in this context that I would like to stress that when presented with accusations or charges that set out to mar a person's character or bring about significant consequences, please let us not be too quick to rush to judgment just because the accuser is perceived or claims to be morally superior to the accused.

My foster parents portrayed my brother to be an evil person simply because of his relentless pursuit of justice. I distinctly remember the day my foster parents returned home after dropping off my brother at Copse and how they explicitly told me that I was better off without my brother. They etched away at his character to the point that, at times, I found myself contemplating whether my brother was, indeed, a bad person. However, after a thorough examination, I could not find any evidence to substantiate my foster parents' fabricated assertions that I was better off without him or he was a bad or evil person.

Prior to being told by the CDA representative that I would be loved and cared for by my foster parents, I thought that only God was capable of demonstrating love, based on what I had been taught (as stated in St. John 3:16) by the charitable organizations that visited the orphanage. After this experience, I found that my understanding of love was not farfetched, because I was able to conclude that only God is capable of demonstrating unconditional love and unwavering compassion. My eyes were open to this truth when I found myself being dropped off at the CDA office like an unwanted animal by the very people who had been entrusted to be my wonderful and loving foster parents. Over the years, I had tried everything possible to save myself from a moment like this, but in the end, there was nothing that I could have done to save myself. Sound familiar? This is also true for the many disenfranchised children who were taught that this world is one big magical kingdom but later found out that such a premise is a false representation of reality.

Despite the emotional trauma that I was going through, I needed to come to terms with reality and realize that my foster parents were long gone and were never coming back. I was now at the mercy of the CDA officers, Ms. Davis and Mrs. Stewart. Irrespective of my emotional tears, Ms. Davis was not yet ready to address my concerns. She was too busy scribbling away in her book. Most likely, she was overwhelmed with everything that had transpired that morning and needed a minute or two

Chapter 1

before soliciting my side of the story. However, at this juncture, it did not matter if my foster parents loved me or not, what really mattered was the fact that this was a day of reckoning and that my foster parents' house had never been meant to be my final destination. Therefore, I needed to stop and think about life in a very conscious way and let God define my destiny.

After Ms. Davis was through, she told me to take my things and place them off to the side. When I reached over and picked up the small cardboard box, she got up out of her chair, peeked over her desk, and said, "Is that all your things? For all the years you have been living with them, you mean to tell me that they could not give you a little bag instead of a cardboard box?" She was even more surprised when she looked inside the box and noticed that there were only two shirts and one pair of pants. Even to this day, I am still unable to figure out why my foster mother kept the rest of my clothes. Well, the only logical explanation is that she was about to make a substantial donation to the Goodwill foundation or some other charitable organization.

Other than the clothes I was wearing, the little cardboard box and its contents were all I had to start out the next chapter of my life. At least this time around, I was not wearing a pair of female shoes. That would have complicated my life even further because, God knows, I had more than enough drama in my life already. In addition to the clothes and the cardboard box, I also had two photographs that I had carried around with me since 1979. One is with my brother and me, and the other is of my former foster mother. Both photographs I have in my possession to this very day.

I know you might be asking, after all the physical and psychological abuse your foster mother inflicted upon you, your brother, and the other children, why would you cherish a photograph of her so dearly that you would have it in your possession even to this very day? Well, if you pose such a question, then you're certainly not alone because many times I have asked myself the very same question but never was able to come up with a definitive answer. However, what I do know is this: For the entire time that I was living with my foster mother, I found myself hoping that someday she would accept me as her son and be that loving and compassionate mother I had been promised. Although that was not the case, over the years I came to realize that my foster mother was not the one who had promised to be a loving and compassionate mother to me. Instead, that was a promise assumed by the CDA representative.

Okay, I should not be too caught up in the nuances of this photograph because there was a long future ahead of me, and the outcome was contingent upon the actions taken by my CDA representative, Ms. Davis. I supposed Ms. Davis had seen enough of my material possessions because she quickly changed the subject and started questioning me regarding the charges that my foster parents had levied against me. First, she said, "Desmond, I am not even going to talk about you sleeping with the girls at the home because I just do not believe that." In hindsight, I should have said, "Ouch! Ms. Davis, you are crushing my manhood. Am I not capable?" Well, I must admit that Ms. Davis was 100 percent correct. Although my foster mother had seen me sleeping at the foot of Debbie's bed, that was all there was to it. Apparently, she had to amplify her accusation to justify her indignation.

Chapter 1

At the time of the incident, I did not realize that there were other meanings to the phrase "sleeping with." In fact, most of my childhood and my adolescence life, I was always sleeping with or sharing a bed with someone because there was never enough for everyone to have his or her own. I hope someday I will have the opportunity to meet up with Debbie so that we can have a good laugh when I share this episode with her. Now that it is in the past, I can make light of what was a very traumatic situation. Once again, I broke down crying uncontrollable tears.

Anyway, after Ms. Davis' had dismissed the "sleeping with the girls" charge, she asked, "What is this I hear about you stealing their money and gambling it away, and running away from home and sleeping out at nights? Desmond, please explain. I need to hear from you because crying is not going to help you now." My foster mother did not disclose to the CDA officers that the money they had accused me of stealing had something to do with me operating their grocery store. Instead, they phrased it in such a way that it appeared as though I had stolen hundreds of dollars from their personal possessions. I can only surmise that they did not want the CDA officers to know that they had me operating their grocery store, especially on days when I should have been in school. I am not sure if I explained the full details of the grocery store robbery to Ms. Davis, but I made it clear to her that I had not stolen any money from my foster parents. As for the gambling part, I did not have the slightest clue what they were talking about because at the time, I did not understand the basic rules of a simple game of cards or dominoes. In fact, I did not learn the make-up of a deck of cards or a pack of dominoes until many years later, when I took my first statistics course.

Moreover, what made my foster mother's accusation rather strange was the fact that the hundreds of dollars she had reported missing had significant monetary value in 1983. This was the main reason why Ms. Davis had interrupted my foster parents and asked them why a child who was not responsible for himself would need so much money. Also, she continued probing by asking them if they had seen any tangible items in my room or anywhere around the house that would substantiate their claim. Unable to provide Ms. Davis with an answer, my foster mother told her that I had gambled it away. Right then and there I detected that Ms. Davis knew that my foster parents' accusation was baseless. Their story simply did not add up. I am quite sure that my foster mother would have thought about her response a little better had she known that Ms. Davis would put the onus on her to prove her case. If it was that easy for me to steal hundreds of dollars from my foster parents, then why would I need to indulge in gambling? Why would I have that much money and then decide to gamble it away just for fun. Even to this day, I have not yet visited Las Vegas because I heard, "When your money goes to Vegas, it stays in Vegas."

Anyway, as for the sleeping out at nights, or should I say the couple of nights that I slept at the neighbor's home, I was guilty but not without a reasonable explanation. I had no other choice because I had been locked out of the house and needed a place to stay. Not only that, but it was obvious that my foster parents' pets were not happy with my camping out on their bed (the little

Chapter 1

wooden bench) at nights. Well, the pets were not one of the reasons, but as you can see, I do have a bone to pick with them for the times they devoured my lifesaver meals.

Now that I have outlined the superficial reasons why my foster parents took me back to the CDA, I will fast-forward and outline what I think is the main reason. On December 9, 2009, while I was at the CDA office in Falmouth, patiently reading through my file, I came across several letters of complaint my foster mother had written to the agency. One such complaint was that I had failed the high school entrance exam (I knew it would come back to haunt me), and several others requesting more money from the agency. However, there was one long complaint that my foster mother had written concerning Mr. Wellington, who had been one of my CDA officers. In this complaint, my foster mother included an incident that involved Mr. Wellington, who, she claimed, had placed her life in danger. She went on to say that because of this incident, she could no longer care for me and would like for the agency to remove me from her care as soon as possible. Even to this day, it is quite difficult for me to understand why my foster mother would direct so much anger toward me based on an incident that involved her, Roy (one of her foster children) and one of the CDA officers. Well, there is a little saying in Jamaica, "If yuh cyaa catch Harry, den catch im shut." ("If you are unable to catch Harry, then try and hold onto his shirt.") Therefore, in this situation, I became the scapegoat. Seeing that I was an eyewitness to the incident that caused my

A Day of Reckoning

foster parents to take such drastic action, I might as well fill you in on the details.[3]

Shortly after Roy had left my foster parents' home, he went to work for another person as a minivan operator. However, while operating the minivan, he was involved in an automobile accident and died. I was quite saddened by this because for the little time I had known him, he had been like an older sibling to my brother and me. Therefore, his passing was quite devastating. On the day of the funeral, my foster parents, Mr. Wellington (CDA officer), and hundreds of other people from the neighboring districts were in attendance. I would presume that Mr. Wellington was also Roy's presiding officer while he was in the care of the CDA. From what I heard, Roy's employer and his friends used their vehicles to transport people to and from the funeral service free of cost. That was when I realized how loved and respected Roy was by the people of the different communities he had served.

My foster father and Mr. Wellington were two of the people chosen to provide the eulogy and tribute at Roy's funeral. The problem started when my foster father, throughout the delivery of the eulogy, stated that if it hadn't been for him and his wife, Roy would have turned out to be a gunman because he was always asking for a toy gun as a child. Not only that, but he continued to levy other allegations and speculations that were deemed very much inappropriate and unfounded. While he spoke, I

---

[3] To bring this experience into context, please refer to "The Return of the Foster Child" segment in volume 2. In this section, I provide you with an overview of Roy, who was my former foster parents' first foster child, and the reason why he had to leave their home and the reason for his return and his final departure.

Chapter 1

could feel the tension in the building. I could hear people whispering, "Not true, not true," while others were doing the "not in agreement" head gesture.

After my foster father was through, Mr. Wellington stepped up to the podium and set the record straight by refuting the correlation that Roy would turn out to be a gunman simply because he had asked for a toy gun as a child. Immediately, cheers erupted from the congregation. My foster parents were so upset that they decided to leave before the conclusion of the funeral proceedings. I remember my foster mother looked directly at me and said, "Yes man, dis a di payback mi get fram di Child Care fi tek care a unnu!" ("Yes man, this is the payback I received from the Child Care system for taking care of you guys!") I did not know what action if any she would take concerning me, so I kept really quiet and did not say a word. Shortly after that incident, she wrote the letter I alluded to earlier to the CDA, stating that the agency should make the necessary arrangements to have me removed from her care.

My question is this: if my foster parents went as far as to request that the CDA remove me from their care, then why had they not taken the initiative and returned me to the agency? Why wait until they were able to fabricate other reasons? Why provide me with false hope? Why lead me to believe that if I only obeyed the rules and performed all my chores to their satisfaction, then everything would be all right? Before this revelation, I spent many years lamenting over the things that I could have done differently to establish a better relationship with my foster parents. However, today I realize that no matter how hard I worked and how well I behaved, nothing would have ever been good enough for my foster parents because their actions were marred by their own vindictive minds.

It is quite clear that my foster parents had other motives that were associated with the CDA. I firmly believe that my foster parents' decision in this regard was a way for them to get back at the CDA. However, I still do not understand why my foster mother did everything possible to deny me the opportunity to be loved and cared for by someone else.

The minute I spoke out against my foster parents' injustice was the very day I reaped the same fate as the rest of the foster children. The lesson I learned from this experience reminds me that we are never beyond the reach of injustice, because injustice has no boundaries. This is also a solemn reminder that the well-being of a child should not, under any circumstances, be used as a political ploy or bargaining measure.

Now that I have provided you with the reason why I was taken back to the CDA, we can forget about the fabricated charges and get back to the day of my reckoning. Given the fact that there were no suitable options pertaining to where I would go and to whom, Ms. Davis ended the conversation and continued with her work. My only concern at that point was to hope and pray that I did not find myself being shipped off to Copse.

Around noon, when the dust settled and my former foster parents were long gone (out of sight but surely not out of mind), I finally came to terms with reality. As I sat down on a wooden bench and gazed out the window, it appeared as though I were looking at the man in the mirror and he was staring helplessly right back at me. However, my thought process was constantly

Chapter 1

being interrupted by the hustle and bustle of the typical morning's activities. It was the Christmas season, and everyone and everything was cashing in on the Christmas frenzy. The streets were filled with everything one could ever imagine. There were sellers and buyers, motor vehicles, handcart vendors, and stray animals and birds, such as pigs, goats, dogs, cats, and chickens. It was as though all the animals from a nearby farm had invaded the town. In addition to all the stray animals, there was a monster goat who was known to everyone as Big Jim. On that particular day, he would come by the window every so often, as if he were asking me for something to eat. Well, that morning, Big Jim was in for a big disappointment because I had nothing to eat and was a lot hungrier than he was.

While I was there reminiscing and contemplating, Ms. Davis came over and began speaking straightforwardly. Let's forget the Jamaican Patois because she was speaking directly to me in plain English. First, she said, "Desmond, I am going to try my best to help you because from the minute I saw you walk through that door, I noticed something special about you. All I have to do now is to try and find you a home." She paused for a couple of seconds then said, "Desmond, my number one priority today is to find you a home."

Shortly after that, she followed up with many questions. First she asked, "Desmond, do you have any idea where your mother or father is?" I replied, "No." Then she asked, "Do you know where any of your brothers or sisters are?" Again, I replied, "No." Lastly she asked, "Do you know of any family member who you could stay with for a while?" Again, I replied, "No." Unfortunately, no

A Day of Reckoning

was the only answer I could provide her regarding the whereabouts of any of my family members. I did not have the slightest clue where my parents or even a distant relative were. Therefore, any thought of being reunited with a family member that day was entirely out of the question.

As I sat helplessly and watched the time ticked away, I could hear Ms. Davis and Mrs. Stewart going over several options of what to do with me. Later that morning, for a second time, Ms. Davis came over and said, "Desmond, I am going to see if someone can keep you until we can work something out." At one point, she even suggested that if she had completed the building of her house, she would have allowed me to stay with her for the interim. That was when I realized that Ms. Davis was genuinely looking out for my well-being.

As the day progressed, the thought of finding a home was quickly replaced by the hunger that was taking a toll on me. However, just before the hunger devoured me, Ms. Davis gave me a couple of dollars and told me to go and buy lunch at the pastry shop that was located in the town square. I thanked her and immediately ran off to the town square. Upon arrival, I forced my way through the crowd (mostly school kids) and placed my order. I bought a patty, a coco bread, and a drink and ran back to the office. Just as I was about to take the first bite from my mouth-watering patty and coco bread sandwich, guess who was right there staring at me? If you guessed Big Jim, then you are absolutely correct. I mean that monster goat was right there looking at me as if he was saying, "Maaay I have a piece?" That day Big Jim was out of luck because I was simply too hungry to

Chapter 1

share my lunch, especially not knowing where my next meal was coming from. I would like to paraphrase Marie Antoinette's "Let them eat cake" phrase by saying, "Let Big Jim eat grass."

After enjoying my first meal of the day, I remained seated on the bench and watched as Ms. Davis and Mrs. Stewart wrapped up their day's work. As the sun began to set beyond the horizon, I noticed that most of the shoppers and the street vendors started leaving town. That was when it dawned on me that everyone was going home except for me. I did not have anyone, not even a distant family member or friend, to go home with. As I sat there, several thoughts started echoing through my mind, and the lonely feeling that had subsided started to overwhelm me once more.

To further complicate the matter, the lyrics of a popular song ("Surround me with love . . .") kept playing over and over in my head. I just could not get those emotional words out of my head. Even throughout the writing of this episode, the words of this song came back to me just as they had done on that day. I was quite curious, so I Googled it and found out that Charly McClain was the artist who sang this sad song. I wonder if she or the songwriters had similar experiences to what I was going through that day. Just a thought.

Witnessing the daylight hours fading away made it appear as though the world was really closing in on me. Only the dark matter theory could explain what I was experiencing. For a second time, I felt the tears coming down my cheeks. However, I realized that this was not the time for me to start crying uncontrollably again. Instead, it was time for me to hope and pray for a way out of my predicament.

A Day of Reckoning

Just before closing, Ms. Davis came over for the third time and said, "Desmond, it is almost closing time. What are we going to do?" Instead of trying to come up with an answer, I just sat there, hoping that it was more of a rhetorical question. I believe that she was merely talking out aloud. Knowing that this was a defining moment of my life, I found myself hoping and praying that I would not find myself being shipped off to Copse.

Ms. Davis followed up by saying, "Desmond, I know this lady who works in the store across the street. I wonder if she would be able to keep you until we can find a home for you." Immediately after that, she got up, hurried out of the office, and went across the street and into Ms. Chen's store. I am not sure if the lady who owned the store was Ms. Chen, but as I have stated before, Jamaicans tend to address most Chinese businesspersons as Mr. or Ms. Chen, regardless of what their real names are. As I sat there on the bench looking out the window, I was hoping and praying that Ms. Davis would return with good news.

The minute I saw Ms. Davis stepped out of the store, I could see the joy and the overwhelming happiness radiating from her face. The minute she arrived, she said, "Desmond, today you are a very lucky man. Ms. Clemmie told me that you can come and stay with her." At that defining moment, my sorrow and my emotional grief were replaced with an everlasting burst of joy. As soon as Ms. Davis was through speaking, I wasted no time. I took up the little cardboard box with my belongings and ran out of the office, across the street, and into the store where I saw Ms. Clemmie. Or, I should say, the person I thought was Ms. Clemmie. I was so happy, I totally forgot that I should have waited for Ms. Davis to accompany me to the

Chapter 1

store and introduce me to Ms. Clemmie. Anyway, the lady was very busy because it was the Christmas season and the store was filled with customers. I wanted to ask her if she was Ms. Clemmie, but I refrained from doing so because I did not want to interrupt her. With that in mind, I stood off to the side and observed as she assisted the customers who were ahead of me with their shopping. Approximately fifteen minutes later, Ms. Davis came into the store and stood by me. The woman took a break from her busy schedule and came over to where we were standing. Wasting no time, Ms. Davis said, "Desmond, here is Ms. Clemmie, the lady who will be taking care of you." After a brief conversation they bid each other goodbye and Ms. Davis left the store. Ms. Clemmie beckoned to me to have a seat on a chair that was located in the waiting area while she attended to the customers.

CHAPTER 2

TRANSITION

Once again, my life was embarking on an entirely new frontier. I was exhausted and hoping that Ms. Clemmie was getting ready to call it a day, but little did I realize that I had a couple of hours to go before closing. Therefore, I had no other choice but to sit there and observe as the customers made their way in and out of the busy store doing their Christmas shopping. Many of the customers had their gifts wrapped by a boy who made his services available to them.

After sitting in the waiting area for approximately three hours, Ms. Chen signaled to Ms. Clemmie that it was time to prepare the store for closing. After the unwanted and misplaced items were removed, folded, and returned to their rightful places, Ms. Chen turned off the operational lights and Ms. Clemmie and I bid her goodnight and walked out of the store together.

On our way to the bus stop, Ms. Clemmie and I indulged in sporadic conversation. I avoided asking her too many questions because, based on her body language, I knew that she was quite exhausted. It was evident because she had just completed a fourteen-hour work shift. After a short walk, we reached the bus depot. The journey was less

Chapter 2

than a quarter of a mile in actual distance, but it appeared much longer because we were both exhausted. We waited for one of the minivans that operated on that route to arrive. We did not have to wait too long because, within ten to fifteen minutes, a minivan arrived at the depot. We went on board, took seats, and waited for the remaining vacant seats to be filled with passengers.

After the minivan was filled beyond the manufacturer's capacity (which is considered normal in Jamaica), the driver came in, honked the horn several times, and sped off in a hurry. The driver made many stops, dropping off passengers along the way. Although I was exhausted, I was unable to take a nap because the passengers kept shouting, "Wan stap, driva" ("One stop, driver"), as the vehicle reached their destinations. After approximately twenty minutes, we arrived at our destination. Ms. Clemmie, whom I had thought was sound asleep, shouted, "Wan stap, driva." I can only conclude that she had a mental picture of the journey and knew exactly when the minivan would arrive at her destination. I had no clue where I was, however, I found out later that Ms. Clemmie was residing at Hague. Before you go off speculating, I would like to make it clear that the Hague in reference is a small residential community located in Trelawny, Jamaica, and not in the Netherlands. Now that I think about it, the Hague in the Netherlands is exactly where I should have gone so that I could have had an opportunity to plead my case. Moreover, its motto ("International city of peace and justice") speaks for itself. Okay, moving on.

It was not until I had an opportunity to compose my autobiography before I really came to terms with the magnitude of Ms. Clemmie's decision. Can you imagine getting up, going to work like usual, and after eight hours of hard work, mostly on your feet you are being presented with a total stranger and being told that such person is now your primary responsibility? When I say responsibility, I am not just referring to someone asking you for a meal or a couple of dollars, but instead, a child of fifteen years old who you have never met or heard of before. So, instead of going home to get a good night's rest, Ms. Clemmie had a whole new responsibility to contend with. For this I could not have been any more grateful, knowing that Ms. Clemmie had a compassionate heart for a total stranger like me.

Home at Last

We had only a couple of feet to walk because Ms. Clemmie's house was within proximity to the road. We navigated our way through the dark to the rear of the house. At the time, I was not sure why she did not use the front door instead of stumbling her way through the dark to the rear of the house, but I found out later that Ms. Clemmie reserved the front entrance for her guests. The moment I stepped into the house, I knew right away that I was at home. It was warm and cozy, none of that cold and lonely feeling that had plagued me while I was living with my former foster parents. Ms. Clemmie then pointed to a room that was adjacent to the kitchen and said, "Desmond, here is where you are going to stay, but you will have to share the room with another young man. His name is Merritt." She went on to say, "He is a bright and mannerly young man, and he goes to the high school down the road." She was referring to the William Knibb Memorial High School that is located in Martha Brae,

Chapter 2

Trelawny.[4] That was all the introduction Ms. Clemmie provided, because time was of the essence and she needed to get going with the dinner preparations.

As soon as the dinner preparation got underway, a boy ran through the door and said, "Good evening, Ms. Clemmie." Ms. Clemmie replied likewise then said, "Merritt, here is a young man who is going to be living with us because he has nobody to take care of him." He replied, "Not a problem, Ms. Clemmie." His reply was spontaneous, with absolutely no reservation whatsoever.

The three of us sat around the dining table and talked as we enjoyed our delicious meals. Wow! Did you hear what I said! Just in case you did not, then let me repeat. I said, all three of us sat at the dining table and enjoyed our delicious meals. Ms. Clemmie did not insist that I go sit outside or at a designated area on the floor. Instead, she offered me a seat at the table. It was a wonderful feeling not to be treated like an outcast. While eating, I was bombarded with many questions: Where had I been living? What happened that I was not living there anymore? What happened to my family? How did I end up in foster care? And many, many more questions for which I did not have the answers or was too tired to talk about. In hindsight, it is not easy for me to fathom that Ms. Clemmie and Merritt would undertake the risk of accepting a total stranger into their home, without knowing who I really was.

---

4 Martha Brae is a little district that it is situated just outside the town of Falmouth, Trelawny. It is well known for its river rafting tourist attraction. Falmouth also hosts one of the more modern ports that accommodate large cruise ships. To top it off, the world's fastest man, Usain Bolt, is also a past student of the William Knibb Memorial High School.

Transition

After dinner, we took turns showering because the house had only one bathroom. Shortly after that, we all retired to bed. Speaking of bed, not only was I sharing Merritt's room, but I had to share his bed as well. The room had one large bed (most likely a king size). However, we had no problem with space, seeing that we were two skinny boys. I was a bit nervous because I was not sure if this was a good idea for me to be infringing on this young man's territory. I was left speechless because Merritt was willing to accept such inconvenience by sharing his room and his bed with a total stranger! I was very grateful because Merritt could have denied me access to his room or even demanded that I sleep on the floor, but instead, he chose to sacrifice his comfort so that I could be comforted. That is why I would like to take this opportunity to express my sincere thanks and gratitude to Merritt for bestowing unto me such an overwhelming act of compassion. Good deeds such as this are very hard to measure with words, but will certainly endure the test of time. I hope that Merritt and I can cross paths again someday so that I can express my sincere thanks and gratitude to him in person.

Although Ms. Clemmie and Merritt had made sacrifices to make me feel at home, the big dilemma was with the living arrangements, which could pose several issues if not addressed soon. One such issue was that Ms. Clemmie would be forced to forfeit her additional source of income (the boarding of students) so that she could care for me. The second issue was what action Merritt's mother would take when she found out that Ms. Clemmie had a total stranger sharing a room with her son. If Merritt's mother did not approve of this arrangement, then Ms.

Chapter 2

Clemmie would be forced to make a very tough decision. Most likely, I would find myself back at the CDA seeking other alternatives. Then the real question would be where I would go and to whom.

Tuesday morning bright and early, I woke up to a "bangarang" noise coming from the kitchen. Ms. Clemmie was shuffling through the pots and pans getting ready to prepare breakfast for Merritt because he had to leave early for school. After Merritt got dressed, he ate his breakfast, bid us goodbye, and went by the roadway to catch a taxi or one of the public passenger minivans that operated on the route. Ms. Clemmie told me that I would be accompanying her to work.

After I was through with breakfast, I got dressed, and Ms. Clemmie and I left together. Because I did not have a job and was not attending school, I had no idea what I was going to do with the next twelve to fourteen hours while Ms. Clemmie was at work. I still had to accompany her because she had not yet developed the level of trust in me to leave me at home.

We boarded a minivan that commuted between Hague and Falmouth. After making many stops, we arrived at the town square. (It should have been called a town circle rather than a town square because it was one giant circle.) Ms. Clemmie and I got off, and she dropped me off at the CDA office before going to work. Once again, the real dilemma for me was finding creative ways to spend the next twelve to fourteen hours.

I greeted Ms. Davis and Mrs. Stewart with a wonderful good morning and a big and pleasant smile, a colossal difference to the doom and gloom trauma I had endured the previous day. Before I settled in, they asked me if I

Transition

was happy to be living with Ms. Clemmie. Although I had deep reservations regarding the living accommodations, I told them that I was happy. I also shared with them the warm welcome that I had received from both Ms. Clemmie and Merritt.

That day, I spent the first eight hours at the CDA office. When the office closed for the day, Ms. Clemmie arranged for me to stay at the police station until she was through working. She knew the police officer who was in charge, so I was allowed to spend the next four to six hours there. After she was through working, we went home and, once again, she went straight to the kitchen and prepared dinner. After we were through with dinner, we chitchatted for a while, with most of the conversation about me. Around 9:30 p.m., Ms. Clemmie retired to bed, and I washed the dishes, including the pots and pans. After dinner, Merritt showered then completed his assignments. I did not have any school-related assignments, so instead of just sitting there watching Merritt, I decided to go to bed early so that I could catch up on some needed sleep. Moreover, after taking a glance at Merritt's textbook, I realized that I did not have the slightest clue what he was doing, because his academic level was light years ahead of mine. From that point forward, that was pretty much the routine for the weekdays.

Before I could gather my thoughts, it was Saturday morning. Everyone slept in late because Ms. Clemmie was not scheduled to work that weekend. Later, we enjoyed a lovely Saturday morning breakfast. If my memory is correct, I believe we hopped over to the nearest Jamaican five star restaurant and ordered a hefty breakfast. Okay, let me be serious and tell you exactly what was for breakfast. Ms.

Chapter 2

Clemmie prepared boiled green bananas, callaloo, saltfish (dried salted cod), and hot Milo. Once again, we sat at the dining table and enjoyed our breakfast. Initially, it was quite difficult for me to accept the fact that Ms. Clemmie would allow me to sit at the table and enjoy a meal with the family.

After breakfast, Ms. Clemmie resorted to her regular weekend chores while Merritt went to the neighbor's home. He spent most of the day at the neighbor's house because he and the neighbor's son were friends, and they both attended the William Knibb Memorial High School. As for me, I stayed home just in case Ms. Clemmie needed my assistance with any of her weekend chores. Moreover, there was no need for me to leave such a warm and cozy home to go anywhere else. Later that afternoon, Ms. Clemmie made a lovely pot of chicken soup and, once again, we all sat at the dining table and enjoyed our dinner. Later that night, somewhere around 9:00 p.m., we retired to bed.

Sunday morning Ms. Clemmie got up and prepared breakfast, then she and I got dressed for church. Merritt did not join us that morning; most likely he went by his friend's home to study. We boarded a minivan to Falmouth and got off at the town square, then walked to the church, which was just a couple blocks from where Ms. Clemmie worked. When compared to the Hope Gospel Chapel that I used to attend with my former foster parents, this was a much larger congregation and had many more children in attendance. This time around, I was not wearing a pair of female shoes, so I was not afraid to associate with the other children. And for that, I would like to say a big Hallelujah! followed by a resounding Amen!

After church, we boarded a minivan and went back home. As soon as we got home, Ms. Clemmie went straight

Transition

to the kitchen to finalize her traditional Jamaican dinner. Please do not forget the detailed explanation I outlined in my previous volume as to how Jamaicans take great pride in the preparation of their Sunday dinners. That Sunday afternoon Ms. Clemmie prepared baked chicken, rice and beans, lots of vegetables, and finally a large jug of real Jamaican juice. Not only that, but Ms. Clemmie also provided me with a nice serving of chicken, nothing like the little scraps my former foster mother would give me. Once again, we sat around the dining table and enjoyed our Sunday dinner.

After we were through with dinner, I assisted Ms. Clemmie with the washing of the dishes, including the pots and pans. Later that afternoon, Merritt invited me to the playground for a game of soccer with him and his friends. I asked Ms. Clemmie for permission before leaving home because I did not want to repeat my former foster parents "out of the yard" drama all over again. Ms. Clemmie replied with a resounding, "Yes, man!" With that said, I accompanied Merritt to the soccer field. However, I watched from the sidelines, because I did not have the proper attire, nor was I up to their caliber. After the game concluded, we went home, showered, and finally retired to bed. Once again, we were getting ready for the beginning of yet another busy week. Well, I should emphasize that the word busy only applied to Ms. Clemmie and Merritt because I had no school and no job. Therefore, my days were quite long and boring.

Instead of repeating the details of my daily routine, I will provide you with a snapshot of the outstanding events. On a normal day, I spend the first eight hours at the CDA office. After the office closed, I would end up camping out

Chapter 2

at the little police station located across from the store where Ms. Clemmie worked. Why did I have to spend an average of four to six hours per day at the constable station? First, I had nowhere else to go after the CDA was closed, and second, Ms. Clemmie knew the police officer (everyone referred to him as Fuzzy) who was in charge. I can assure you that it was quite boring for me to spend that many hours sitting on a wooden bench in a police station. However, an occasional drama or two would unfold and liven up the place a bit. Also, I did get to watch a number of police operations as they unfolded, although most of the time they were a bit overdramatized by Fuzzy.

Here is how Fuzzy would go about executing his takedown operations. The first interesting event unfolded one day when Fuzzy received a call on the radio informing him that there were two young men wreaking havoc for shoppers all over the town. The pickpockets were going around the town snatching men's billfolds and women's purses. This practice was common throughout the holiday seasons, especially during the Christmas holidays. Before executing this particular operation, Fuzzy drank two shots of rum, and then said to his partner, "Mek wi guh get di [expletive] pickpocket bwoy dem." ("Let us go and apprehend the [expletive] pickpocket boys.") I sneaked out of the station behind Fuzzy, but stayed a good distance so as not to be seen by him and or his partner. That day the drama ended with Fuzzy giving the criminals a wedgie ("drape them up," as we say in Jamaica) and made them walk from where they were apprehended through the busy town and finally to the station. His philosophy was to embarrass them as much as he could so that it would deter others from participating in such unlawful behavior.

Transition

I am not sure why or who tagged the chief constable with this pet name. However, knowing Jamaicans, it might have been because he drank a lot of alcohol and probably did not think clearly during such times. Fuzzy was one heck of a comedian, but he seemed to get the job done no matter what the circumstances were.

Seeing that your memory is far better than mine, you should remember the monster goat I alluded to earlier. Just in case you forgot, this goat was known as Big Jim to everyone who lived in Falmouth and the neighboring districts. Big Jim was no ordinary goat. First, he did not eat grass like other goats. No sir! He only ate patties, coco bread, snacks, and other bad LDL cholesterol food. Not only that, but after eating all that junk, one would think that Big Jim would drink his recommended daily twelve ounces of water. I am here to say, that was simply not the case. He would go by the constable's office every so often because he knew that Fuzzy would give him his regular dose of alcoholic beverages such as Jamaican rum, Guinness, Heineken, and Dragon Stout. Big Jim was highly addicted to every form of alcoholic beverage known to man. After consuming the alcohol, Big Jim would end up chasing women down the street as they passed by the constable's station. You would hear the women who were being chased screaming, "Constable, Constable, cum get dis yah renkin goat fram mi yuh hear sah!" ("Constable, come and remove this urine-odor smelly goat away from me!") Well, have no fear "little lady" because Fuzzy was always there to the rescue. Fuzzy would take up his baton, walk right up to Big Jim, and give him a good whack. Big Jim would immediately stop the messing around, make a U-turn, and accompany Fuzzy right back to the station as if he knew he had been caught doing something wrong.

Chapter 2

Another one of Big Jim traits was the fact that he had no fear; I mean, zero fear or regard for Ms. Chen and her employees. On several occasions, he walked straight into Ms. Chen's supermarket, helped himself to a snack, and walked right out of the store. Here is how Big Jim would execute his snack-snatching operation. First, he would go by the roadway and look in both directions. Second, after the way was clear, he would walk across the road and make his way up the steps into Ms. Chen's supermarket. Third, he would help himself to whatever snacks were within his reach, and walk right out of the store. Let me repeat, Big Jim would walk right out of the store without paying for the items he had taken. He did not even consider joining the express checkout queue. The actions of this goat constituted the most blatant form of shoplifting, perpetrated in broad daylight. The most hilarious part was that while Big Jim was on his way out of the store, I could hear Ms. Chen shouting, "Get out of here! You damn goat! Get out of here!" However, none of her screaming and ranting deterred Big Jim. Instead of running away, Big Jim would just keep on walking until he was back at the police station. As soon as he found a comfortable spot, he would lie down, remove the wrappings, and enjoy his delicious snack. Not only that, but Big Jim did not consider sharing his delicious snacks with me. No sir! He simply returned the favor because I did not offer him any of my patty and coco bread.

One day I witnessed Big Jim going into Ms. Chen's store and, within a couple of seconds, rushing out with a bar of washing soap in his mouth. Not sure why he was in such a hurry that day. Anyway, after taking two nibbles from the bar of soap, he figured out that it was not

Transition

something edible. I do believe that Ms. Chen replaced the snacks on the lower shelves with bars of soap just to teach Big Jim a lesson. Irrespective of the soap drama, Big Jim was a very clever goat. He would roam the town throughout the day, but as soon as the sun began to set, he would lie down at the entrance of the police station. He did so to avoid becoming Jamaican curry goat. With all the crimes that Big Jim had committed, one would think that Fuzzy would have slapped the cuffs on him and hauled him off to jail. But that was simply not the case. Instead, he let Big Jim act as though he was above the law.

Anyway, that was pretty much my daily routine, including the dramas orchestrated by Fuzzy and Big Jim. This is what happens when a person has too much idle time. After approximately three weeks, Ms. Clemmie had developed enough trust in me to allow me to stay home while she was at work. I was very grateful for this opportunity, because I no longer had to get up Monday through Friday and go into the town with no real sense of purpose. It was not so much the trip, but the long and hungry days I had to spend away from home.

Due to financial constraints, Ms. Clemmie was unable to provide me with three meals per day. Throughout those days, it appeared as though I were going through eternity before my next meal. After breakfast was served (approximately 6:30 a.m.), I had to wait until 7:00 p.m., and sometimes even 9:00 p.m., for my next meal. She tried her best to provide me with fruit, such as orange, grapefruit, or a finger or two of ripe banana for lunch. However, she would make up for lunch with a hefty dinner, which was always "better late than never." Although I was no longer roaming the town, my main concern was the consistent

Chapter 2

boredom I had to go through five days per week. This lifestyle was even more apparent considering that I had always been busy from 6:00 a.m. to 8:00 p.m., and sometimes 10:00 p.m., while living with my former foster parents. Now that I was living with Ms. Clemmie, this busy schedule abruptly ended, and life felt as though it were at a standstill. Little had I realized how my mind and body were conditioned for a busy day's routine.

The Value of Work

After a couple of weeks of doing absolutely nothing, Ms. Clemmie provided me with some good news. She had secured me a holiday job with the public works department (parish council). I was very excited, especially knowing that I would finally be putting my time to productive use. I could hardly wait for Monday morning so that I could get started.

Finally, it was Monday morning! I got up bright and early, showered, dressed, and boarded a minivan destined for the town of Falmouth. I was getting ready to undertake my first state-of-the-art, real-world job. Okay, I must admit that I had no idea regarding my job function. Therefore, I should not have assumed that it was definitely going to be the most glamorous job. However, any job was far better than just sitting at home or roaming the town day after day with no real sense of purpose.

Upon arrival, a pleasant young woman greeted me and told me to follow her. I followed her down the hallway and into an open area where several women were typing away on their rather noisy typewriters. She showed me a large box filled with documents and told me that my job was to shred them into small pieces. Aha! I know what you are thinking. You are assuming that this was an easy job because all I had to do was to feed the thousands of pages into a giant shredder that was made available to me. To that I say, think again! There was no such thing as a shredder! Actually, I have been designated as the public works human shredder. I had to shred volumes and volumes of papers with my bare hands all day long.

Once again, shredding documents was far better than roaming the streets or spending several hours at home or inside a police station with absolutely nothing to do. Moreover, this task was a piece-of-cupcake job compared to the enormous amount of work I had been accustomed to while living with my former foster parents. Therefore, with a big smile on my face, I sat down and started shredding away at the volumes of papers that were piled up before me. I remember saying to myself, "This is easy!" I could see myself doing this all week long while displaying a "no problem, man" work attitude. However, after the first four hours, my fingers started giving me a burning sensation. I had done quite a lot of manual chores while living with my former foster parents, but shredding paper was not one of them. It was obvious that I had not built up any resistance to this task.

After the third day, my shredding fingers were numb, which meant I was no longer feeling the aches and pains I had felt the previous two days. I managed to survive the week with all my fingers intact. At the end of the week, Ms. Clemmie collected my pay and used her big employee discount to purchase some clothing and other necessities for me. My first reaction was, "Wow! With this much attire I think I am going to need a bigger cardboard box."

Chapter 2

I wish I had another two weeks of this work, but I was not so fortunate. Anyway, life goes on, and the routine I explained above, except for the week that I worked for the public works department, was pretty much the norm.

However, I was continually juggling around ideas in my head regarding finding a permanent foster parent. One day while I was all alone at home, a breakthrough in the form of a megawatt light bulb came on inside my head. That was when the bright light revealed Aunt Lucy as the person who had been ordained by the Lord to become my foster mother. Before I proceed with this segment, I would like to let you know that, despite what I am about to say concerning this outcome, I truly believe that this revelation was a divine intervention from the Lord and not of my own accord. My only explanation is that the Lord used my *then* to bring me to my *now*.

The Connection

You might be asking, so who is this Aunt Lucy person? Was she one of my biological family members? No, she was not a family member. However, one thing I am most certain of is that this total stranger has been more to me than any of my biological family members. Although I gave you a brief overview of Aunt Lucy in the introductory section, I would like to provide you with a quick refresher of this wonderful person I met along life's journey.

Aunt Lucy resided in Sawyers, which is a little farming district located in the parish of Trelawny. Although everyone (the very young to the golden oldie) from the community addressed this wonderful person as Aunt Lucy, her real name was Fredricka Brady. While I was

Transition

living with my former foster parents, I was privileged to attend the Hope Gospel Hall, also located in Sawyers. Aunt Lucy was also a member of this church. I was not drawn to her because she was a member of this church, but instead, I was drawn to her because I always looked forward to the snacks and other tasty treats she would provide us.

Here is how a typical church-day visit to Aunt Lucy's home would unfold. Aunt Lucy used to operate a little grocery shop that was located less than a mile away from the church. With this at the forefront of our minds, we (the children) would sneak out of the church before the service commenced and run to Aunt Lucy's home, knowing that she would never send us away empty-handed. The minute we arrived, we would bang away at her door. Aunt Lucy would come out and scold us by saying, "Listen to mi, man! Why aren't you young people in church? Why are you out here beating down my door?" After Aunt Lucy was through speaking, we would reply, "We are here for some water, Aunt Lucy." She would go back inside the house, and sure enough, she would return with a jug filled with water, along with an assortment of candies and snacks. She would pour each of us a glass of water, and after we were through drinking, she would then give us the snacks and say, "Come on man, unnu get back to church now, you hear me?" As for me, it was not just about the water or the snacks, but instead, it was about the lifetime connection that Aunt Lucy and I had made without any of us realizing it at the time.

Now that I have told you how I came to know Aunt Lucy, it is time to get back to the day when she became the focal point of my thought process. God had revealed

Chapter 2

unto me my foster mother, but I was in need of a way to establish communication with her. Well, that was easy because all I had to do was to pick up "di iPhone and have Siri deliver a message fe di I." Just kidding, there was no such communication device back then. At the time, neither Aunt Lucy nor Ms. Clemmie had telephones. Therefore, delivering my message was only possible in person, through word of mouth, or by the post office.

After thinking it over, I decided that visiting her in person would be the most compelling of the three options. However, I was now faced with the task of coming up with the most appropriate way to convince Ms. Clemmie that I need to take a trip to Sawyers. After juggling several options in my head, I finally found one that I thought would work. I told her that I had gotten an invitation to visit the Hope Gospel Hall church I used to attend while I was living with my former foster parents. Liar, liar, pants, shirts, and the little cardboard box were all on fire. Well, I had not really received an invitation; I sort of invited myself. Anyway, with some reservations, Ms. Clemmie asked why. I told her that it was a special Sunday service and that I would like to attend. After she listened to what I had to say, I could see that she was quite concerned and a bit hesitant to grant me permission. However, after a long pause, she finally gave me permission.

I was very happy because this trip would provide me with the opportunity to ask Aunt Lucy if she would consider becoming my foster mother. Well, seeing that Aunt Lucy did not have much, it would be more like asking her to provide me with life's essentials, such as food, shelter, and clothing in exchange for me doing her manual labor. It was more like becoming her yard boy. In other words, I was desperately in need of a foster mother so that I would avert a possible tough decision to be made by Ms. Clemmie in the near future. That is, she would no longer have to give up her additional source of income of providing room and board for students.

In Search of a Foster Parent

The long-awaited Sunday morning had finally arrived, and with much enthusiasm I got up, showered, dressed, and walked approximately one mile to the bus stop. Within fifteen to twenty minutes, the bus (most likely it was one of the King Alphonso buses) arrived, and I waved my hand vigorously to get the driver's attention. The driver stopped the bus, and I hurried on board and made myself comfortable. I was feeling very optimistic regarding the outcome of this trip. Moreover, I was on my way to attend a service at the *Hope* Gospel Hall church. So, having hope and lots of optimism, what could possibly go wrong?

Well, if you stick around long enough, you will find out that the old Murphy's law is about to teach me a fine lesson. After a long and bumpy ride, I finally made it to Sawyers. I decided that instead of going directly to the Hope Gospel Hall, I would first stop off at Aunt Lucy's home. She was the reason I had made the trip in the first place. As soon as the bus arrived at Aunt Lucy's home, I rang the bell, and the driver stopped the bus. With much haste, I disembarked, and, with a few steps, I made my way to Aunt Lucy's house. This took me less than a minute because Aunt Lucy's home is so close to the main road that when I stepped off the bus, I only had to take an additional three or four steps.

Chapter 2

At first glance, I did not see Aunt Lucy or her cousin, Sister Lin. I knew that they were somewhere inside the house because the passageway and the dining room doors were wide open. Within a couple of minutes, Aunt Lucy came into the dining room. She was very surprised to see me. I remember she said, "Desmond, is that you? What are you doing here, man?"

"Just visiting for the day, Aunt Lucy," I replied. I also told her that I was there to attend the church service. Yeah right! I was not there "to just visit" or "to just attend a special church service." Instead, I was there to ask her if she would be kind enough to provide me with food, clothing, and shelter. In other words, I needed a lifetime of help, and Aunt Lucy was my only hope. However, I blew it on my first attempt. I developed cold feet and simply could not find the courage just to come out and let her know the real reason why I was there. Aunt Lucy is a very smart, rational, and logical thinker, and when you think you have one slipped by her, she has you read like a book. She knew right away that I was making up a story, which was obvious, but she gave me the benefit of the doubt regardless.

After listening carefully to what I had to say, she told me to have a seat. I did accordingly, and she went into the kitchen and prepared a delicious breakfast for me, which I enjoyed gratefully. Aunt Lucy did not have to ask me if I was hungry because she could see the hunger expressions all over my face. Probably she heard the rumbling coming from my stomach as well.

After breakfast, Aunt Lucy, Sister Lin, and I had a short discussion. My former foster parents and Aunt Lucy attended the same church, so I am quite sure that by

Transition

now they had updated her on every detail of why they had taken me back to the CDA. Based on what had happened to my brother, I do believe that none of the church members were expecting to see or hear from me again. With that said, Aunt Lucy pressed on with a couple of questions. She really wanted to find out why I would have traveled from so far away just to attend a regular church service. Aunt Lucy knew that it was highly unlikely that a child of around fifteen years old (my age was not known at the time) would display that much interest in wanting to be at a church service. Once again I stuck to my story.

At approximately 9:45 am, Aunt Lucy signaled to me that it was time to go to church. I walked the less than the quarter of a mile to the church. So far, I had talked about everything except what I really was there to talk about. Nonetheless, I convinced myself that immediately after church, I would let Aunt Lucy know the reason for my trip. As soon as I stepped into the church building, I could see that the church members were surprised to see me. With no hesitation, they started directing many questions at me. They asked me if my former foster parents had taken me back, if I was now living in Sawyers, and whom I was there to see. I told them that I was currently residing at Hague and that I was only visiting for the day. A couple of minutes later, my former foster parents arrived. As soon as they came into the building, they were surprised, and I mean really surprised, to see me. I knew that they would be because I was the last person whom they were expecting to see or hear from that Sunday morning. I did not have any in-depth conversation with them at the moment, but I do remember they asked the reason for my visit and where I was currently living.

Chapter 2

After the morning service, I said goodbye to everyone, including my former foster parents. Shortly after that, I accompanied Aunt Lucy back to her home. Up to this point, I had not yet asked Aunt Lucy the one and only one question that had caused me to travel the long journey from Hague to Sawyers. The bus was scheduled to arrive somewhere between 5:00 p.m. and 6:30 p.m., which meant that I had a good six hours remaining, so there was no need to panic. Well, at least for now.

Later that afternoon, Aunt Lucy offered me a very delicious, traditional Jamaican Sunday dinner. Aunt Lucy, Sister Lin, Brother Sommers (the pastor), and I ate dinner and talked for a while. By the way, I was allowed to sit with the family at the dining table, not outside or in the corner somewhere on the floor. Even throughout our casual conversation, I still could not find the courage or the will just to come out and let Aunt Lucy know that I was there to ask if she would consider becoming my foster mother. Precious time was ticking away, and I had not yet accomplished my goal. I was hoping and praying just to have a couple of minutes alone with Aunt Lucy so that I could convey my desire to her. Well, none of that really happened because before I knew it, I could hear the bus horn echoing through the mountains. Although I heard the bus horn loud and clear, I pretended not to. That was when Aunt Lucy looked at me and said, "Desmond, your bus is coming. Yuh need to go by the roadway now." I got up reluctantly, stepped down the one step that led to the hallway, walked out the door, and finally across the street. I was walking with heavy feet because I simply did not want to leave.

What was I thinking? If I had ten hours to get something done and did not, then what rational explanation did

Transition

I have to convince myself that I could get it done in just a couple of minutes? Within the next two to three minutes, the bus came roaring around the corner. I signaled to the driver by waving my hand (not as vigorously as I had earlier that morning), and the driver pulled over. Before getting on board, I waved goodbye to Aunt Lucy, Sister Lin, and Brother Sommers one last time. I was confused; my mind was telling me to get off the bus and run back to Aunt Lucy's home and let her know that I needed her help. However, it was too late because the bus was full speed ahead.

Lost Opportunity

Now what? I was very disappointed knowing that I had squandered away my golden opportunity. I could not stop thinking about how I had gone all the way from Hague to Sawyers and was now on my way back to Hague without accomplishing my one and only objective. Now I know why Moses needed Aaron to speak on his behalf (Biblical reference). After a long, bumpy, and depressing ride, I finally arrived at Hague. As I started walking along the road, I could not stop thinking how stupid I had been for allowing this opportunity to slip away from me. And how I should have been straightforward, letting Aunt Lucy know precisely why I had come to see her instead of fabricating other reasons. In hindsight, I wish Aunt Lucy had said, "Desmond, this is not the reason why you are here! Let me know exactly why you are really here!"

After the long walk, I finally made it home. I was tired, exhausted, and disappointed. As soon as I stepped through the door, Ms. Clemmie greeted me with a pleasant, "You are home." Immediately she started asking me

Chapter 2

many questions regarding my trip. She asked about the church members, and if they were happy to see me; about the church sermon; and several more questions. Based on my responses and body language, it was quite apparent to Ms. Clemmie that I was not in an enthusiastic mood. She got the hint and refrained from asking me any more questions. I guess she really wanted to find out if I had attended church or went somewhere else. She offered me dinner, but I told her that I was not hungry because I had already eaten. Moreover, I was too disappointed and was in no mood for a second helping. With that said, I took a shower and went straight to bed.

The minute I opened my eyes, I was once again reminded that I was still in need of a place to live. Seeing that I had thrown away a golden opportunity, the real question was how I would get another chance to see Aunt Lucy again, and even if I did, would I find the courage to ask for her help in such regard. While I was at home pondering, the days were going by, and Christmas was fast approaching. Ms. Clemmie and I were the only two people at home because Merritt had gone home to spend the Christmas holiday with his family.

Before I knew it, the Christmas season was over and the New Year was just around the corner. However, I had not yet resolved my living accommodation problem. The school break was also coming to an end, which meant that Merritt and his mother would show up any day. Not only that, but what if Merritt had already told his mother that he was sharing his room with a total stranger? Therefore, if not addressed quickly, this living arrangement could also turn out to be problematic for both Ms. Clemmie and the CDA as well.

Transition

The following morning, I went to the CDA office and told Ms. Davis about this kind lady who lived in Sawyers, was not married, and did not have any children of her own. I told her that I was quite sure that if I asked her permission, she would be delighted to let me come and stay with her. I continued by providing Ms. Davis with details of how I had come to know her, the type of person she was, and how she was well known and well respected by the residents of the Sawyers district. After overhearing my conversation, Mrs. Stewart intervened and said, "I pass through Sawyers every day on my way to and from work." Right then and there I knew that things were moving in the right direction. Without further hesitation, I asked Mrs. Stewart for a pen and a sheet of paper and wrote something to the effect of:

> Aunt Lucy, I am in need of a place to stay and I am asking if I can come and stay with you.
> Thank you, Aunt Lucy.
> From Desmond

After composing my little note, I handed it to Mrs. Stewart. She took the note, and after reading it, she said, "I thought you were giving me the directions, because I will do the talking for you." I told her that the house was located in the Burke district, and it had a little shop at the front facing the main road. She replied, "Oh! I know exactly where it is." However, I pleaded with her to please deliver my hand-written note to Aunt Lucy. Although I did not explain to her why it was important to provide Aunt Lucy with my hand-written note, I surmised that she understood that it was a way for me to express my

Chapter 2

personal desire to Aunt Lucy. Mrs. Stewart assured me that she would do accordingly.

After all was said but not yet done, Ms. Davis looked at me and said, "Desmond, why do you want to leave Ms. Clemmie?" Instead of explaining to Ms. Davis the living accommodation issue, I resorted to the inconsequential stuff. I told her that after breakfast, I did not get anything to eat (except a grapefruit or an orange) until dinner was served. Although this was a true statement, it was evident that being single and living off a small income meant that Ms. Clemmie did not have the financial means to provide me with the care she desired. I was not sure how my reply came across; however, both Ms. Davis and Mrs. Stewart understood that there was a genuine reason why I did not want to stay with Ms. Clemmie any longer. From that point forward, I felt very optimistic regarding the outcome. I could hear a little voice in my head telling me that everything was going to be all right. I had a strong feeling that Aunt Lucy was going to say yes.

Irrespective of my optimism, I was unable to sleep because I was anxiously awaiting daybreak. The next day, immediately after breakfast, I set out on foot from Hague to Falmouth. Upon arrival, I ran straight into the CDA office. The minute I arrived, Ms. Davis told me that Aunt Lucy had given her approval and assured her that I was welcome to come and live with her. Ladies and gentlemen of the known world, I needed no other scientific proof to assure you that I was the happiest person alive that day. I was so overwhelmed with joy. I felt as though my feet were no longer touching the ground.

Not only had God provided for me a home and a foster mother, but my mind was now at peace. Even to this very day, it is still inconceivable for me to fathom the depth, breadth, and height of that defining moment. The moment in which I was given a second chance to life and the pursuit of happiness! This outcome erased any possibility of me being taken to the dreaded Copse juvenile correctional institution. No longer would I have to worry about where to live or what would have happened if the CDA had been unable to find me a permanent home and someone to care for me. Although at the time I was only fifteen years old, I am here to say unequivocally that this experience caused me to stop and think about the true meaning of life in an entirely new way. I could not find enough words to say thank you to Mrs. Stewart and Ms. Davis for the hard work, effort, and dedication that they had put forth on my behalf.

That evening I ran home and packed my belongings. Wait a minute; forget the packing part, because it did not take much effort to pack a little cardboard box. The minute Ms. Clemmie came home, I told her that I had found a church sister who was willing to let me come and live with her. I also told her that I would be leaving in the morning. Ms. Clemmie looked at me in a surprised manner, and rightfully so. I had never mentioned anything to her about leaving or having a need to find a foster parent. From the expression on her face, it was evident that Ms. Davis had not yet spoken with her either. Although I did not outline the details of why I was leaving, I did assure her that I was not leaving because she had done anything wrong. I sincerely believed that Ms. Clemmie realized that I was very much concerned with the accommodations, but she did not question my decision. Although she sounded really sad, she said, "Desmond, I wish you could stay, but it's your decision, and I wish you all the best."

Chapter 2

Despite feeling a bit sad, I was happy because I knew that this decision would work out in the best interests of everyone. Moreover, if Merritt's mother did not approve of the living arrangements, then Ms. Clemmie would have no choice but to have one of us removed from her home.

However, all that was now behind me. That was the last conversation Ms. Clemmie and I had regarding my leaving. That evening, Ms. Clemmie prepared a delicious meal for me. It appeared as though she went all out to give me the best sendoff meal ever. After dinner, I did the dishes and then Ms. Clemmie and I talked for a while, with most of the conversation centered around her adding another room to her house. I knew she was implying that if she had another bedroom, the outcome would have been different. This was not the first time she had discussed the possibility of expanding her home. Moreover, if she had the financial resources, it would have been done already because the house had only two bedrooms. In addition to not having the ideal accommodations, I certainly would not want to disrupt the motherly bond that Ms. Clemmie and Merritt shared, which was far different from what I had witnessed and experienced between my former foster mother and the children who were boarding at her home.

Ms. Clemmie changed the subject and asked me if I had packed my things, to which I replied that I had. When she looked in the corner of the room and saw the little cardboard box, she said, "Where are you going with that cardboard box, man? Let me get you a bag." She went inside her room and, moments later, returned with a nice traveler's bag and handed it to me. I quickly transferred my things from the little USPS "if it fits it ships" cardboard box to a first-class traveler's bag. After we were through talking, we both retired to bed. That night I got approximately two hours of sleep. I was anxiously awaiting the dawn of a new day.

The following morning, I got up and dressed, but decided to take some time to think about the next phase of my life's journey. My thought process was interrupted when Ms. Clemmie went into the kitchen to prepare breakfast. I told her that I needed to get going and that I did not have sufficient time for breakfast. However, she insisted that I have a cup of tea. After drinking the tea, I took my bag, said goodbye to Ms. Clemmie, and went through the door. Just before I went through the gate, Ms. Clemmie bid me one final farewell. Merritt was still home with his family, so I was unable to say goodbye to him. Indeed, this was quite a painful moment for me. However, despite everything that had taken place in my life up to that point, I genuinely believe that the outcome of having Aunt Lucy as my foster mother was the divine intervention of God that was destined to be.

Before I proceed to the next chapter of my life, I would like to share with you the final chapter of Ms. Clemmie's life. First, I really appreciated the fact that Ms. Clemmie had taken on such an enormous responsibility to care for me. Despite her limited resources, she took me into her home and provided for me in every way possible. It was a sad decision for me when I had to leave, but at the same time, I was happy knowing that I would no longer be a burden to her, even though she did not see it that way. While living with Aunt Lucy, I would visit with Ms. Clemmie at her workplace every time that I had an opportunity to go to Falmouth. I would run into her workplace to see her and to find out how things were going with her

Chapter 2

and Merritt. She always welcomed me with a big smile, open arms, a cold refreshing drink, and a little snack. She always filled me in on Merritt's progress and other important events.

I cannot forget the day I went to Falmouth and ran into her workplace to see her and to talk with her as I usually did. Instead of being greeted with her smile and open arms, I was told that she no longer worked there. I inquired the reason, and that was when one of her coworkers told me that she had passed away. I was deeply saddened by the news because I did not know that she had taken ill since my last visit, which was approximately four to six months prior. One thing I can say with all surety is this: Ms. Clemmie's overwhelming compassion will never be forgotten. May her soul find comfort, knowing that she has done well.

CHAPTER 3

THE ALPHA (α)

On the 14th of January, 1984, I departed Hague and commenced my journey to be home with my foster mother, Ms. Fredricka "Lucy" Brady. After bidding Ms. Clemmie goodbye, I hurried to the bus stop because I had but a couple of minutes before the arrival of the bus that operated on the Montego Bay-Mandeville route. As soon as the bus was within proximity, I waved my hand with a sense of urgency to signal to the driver that I needed to board the bus.

The Unforgettable Journey

Once again, I found myself embarking on yet another phase of life's journey. Although I could not say with all certainty, a soothing voice deep within my soul kept reminding me that this was my final destination. Throughout this phase of my journey, I was not being accompanied by any of the CDA officers. Neither was I being snatched away by the police and shuttled off to the unknown. Nor was I being dropped off at the CDA office like an unwanted animal. This time was different. This time I knew exactly where I was going and to whom. This time I could feel

Chapter 3

the presence of the Lord guiding me through what would become my final childhood journey. I can assure you that I was never alone then, nor am I alone now, because God was and is always with me. And having that assurance made the trip even the more comforting.

This journey signified the beginning of a new life and one that had exceeded my wildest imagination. Not because Aunt Lucy had promised me any material wealth or a wonderful academic career, but the mere fact that I would be living with a foster parent of my choosing. When compared with my former foster parents, Aunt Lucy possessed very little material wealth. However, she proved in every way possible, that we can achieve a lot more even when presented with a lot less. In a very humbling way, I really have to give God the glory for giving me the faith, courage, strength, and determination to always hope for a brighter tomorrow. Unfortunately, my brother never had someone like Aunt Lucy to provide him with the love and compassion he yearned for every day of his life.

As the bus ventured through the winding roads that lead to the little farming district of Sawyers, I could not help but think of my new home and how my life was about to be completely transformed. As time progressed and the many thoughts kept buzzing around in my head, I was not worried in the least, because I was confident that today's bus ride was going to be a good one. However, the many people that relied on the bus to transport their farm produce kept prolonging the journey.

Regardless of the extended delays, the bus confidently made its way through the little towns and villages. That morning, we did not encounter any engine problems or have to change any flat tires. Neither did we have to worry

The Alpha (α)

about any of the passengers' produce falling off the bus. After making our way through the different towns, we arrived at Sawyers. Finally, after eight to ten more minutes, the bus arrived at Burke, where Aunt Lucy lived.

Finally, Home

As soon as the bus came to a stop, I stepped off and waved goodbye to the driver. I hurried into the hallway and then into the dining room, where I met Aunt Lucy. There we were, standing face to face. She greeted me with a pleasant "Good morning," and I replied "Good morning, Aunt Lucy!" She then said, "Desmond, listen to mi man! I want you to listen to me real good. You asked me to help you, and that is exactly what I am going to do! You hear mi, man? That is exactly what I am going to do. But you have to want this help. You hear mi, man? You have to be the one who want this help!" Then she went on to say, "Desmond, I am not working anymore, but I am going to try my best. You hear mi, man? I am going to try my best to help you!"

In a calm voice, she said, "Desmond, I have heard many things from . . ." She was referring to my former foster parents. "But I am willing to put all of it behind. You hear mi, man? I mean, all of it. And I want you to do the same. Do you hear mi, man? I want you to do the same." She ended the conversation by saying, "Desmond, I want you to promise yourself. You hear mi, man? Promise yourself that you will turn a clean page. Do you hear mi, man?" After she was through, I remember giving her one resounding "Yes, Aunt Lucy" response to all of her questions and concerns. And that ended what I would describe as our welcome-home dialog.

Chapter 3

In hindsight, I am very grateful that Aunt Lucy was very logical, practical, and straightforward in her conversation regarding what I had requested of her and what she would do for me if I were sincere. I am happy she did not go off repeating the usual emotional words or phrases such as "Desmond, I am going to help you because I Love You and I am going to be that Loving and Caring mother you never had." Most likely I would have been really skeptical because "loving and caring foster parents" were the words used by the CDA representative just before my brother and I were transferred to a life of physical and psychological torment.

After fifteen years of being tossed about like an object in turbulent waters, I was extremely happy to have finally found a resting place. It was as if someone had removed all the worries of this world from my shoulders. I was lost for words because that day, I had witnessed human compassion being demonstrated in its purest form. With such a wonderful feeling radiating deep within my soul, Aunt Lucy did not have to convince me anymore regarding my destiny. I had already made up my mind, and that day signified not just a new page but an entirely new book of life. God knows I did not want to be bound by the old book of life anymore. I had more than enough and was hoping and praying for a normal life. Before I begin the final phase of my childhood journey, I would like to paraphrase Dr. Martin Luther King Jr. by saying, "Home at last! Home at last! Thank God Almighty! I am home at last!"

Now that I was home, what were my real expectations? Knowing what I knew then, I was not asking Aunt Lucy to bestow upon me her love, affection, or any other intangibles that a parent would bestow upon her own child. Moreover, how could I have asked for something that I had no knowledge of or had never experienced before? Neither was I asking Aunt Lucy to provide me with the means necessary to further my academic or professional career. All I was asking of Aunt Lucy was for her to provide me with life's essentials and nothing more. I was simply asking for food, clothes, and shelter.

Seeing that I had nothing to offer her in return, all I could do was to promise her that I would take care of her farm (more like a home garden) and her household chores. The term that was used for this arrangement is that I would become Aunt Lucy's yard boy. In other words, I was simply trading manual labor for life's basic needs. However, Aunt Lucy did not view it that way. She did not say to me, "Desmond, please wait here while I go and crunch the numbers to figure out if it is economically feasible for me to provide for you or not." Neither did she make her decision based on how much economic value she could extract from the CDA or how much manual labor I could provide her in return. I am here to say unequivocally that Aunt Lucy did not indulge in any of those unjust practices. Instead, her desire to care for me was driven by a deep sense of compassion that was rooted in sincere love, not driven by any personal gain.

Here is a little recap and also a peek into the future regarding Aunt Lucy as a parent. Aunt Lucy was born March 23, 1915, and was two months shy of her sixty-ninth birthday at the time she became my foster mother. She had never married nor had any children of her own. However, she had helped with the parenting of other family members, including nieces, nephews, and grand- and great-grandnieces and nephews. In addition to helping her family, she helped many strangers, and I was one of the many strangers who benefited from her overwhelming compassion.

Compare and Contrast Foster Parents

Before I continue, I would like to fast forward to the future as a way to compare and contrast Aunt Lucy's parenting approach with that of my former foster parents'. This will highlight how social, religious, economic, and political aspects influenced their behavior. First, Aunt Lucy's communication methods cut directly across the grain of what I was accustomed to with my former foster parents, more so my former foster mother. Aunt Lucy's parenting style took on a more logical approach; one I understood clearly. Here is a typical example. One day Aunt Lucy sat me down for a little parent-to-child conversation. Throughout our discussion, she said to me, "Desmond, when I talk to you I want you to listen to mi. You hear mi, man? I want you to listen to mi. But I also want you to let me know what is on your mind regarding what I have said. If I tell you to pick up that broom from inna di corner and put it outside, I am expecting you to do just that. But if I come back later and you did not pick up di broom, den I am going to remind you. But if I come back again and di broom is still there, den we need to talk. Yes, we are going to talk because you might have a better reason why di broom should remain there. But you have to let me know because if you don't, den I am going to think that you don't want to listen." Then she went off into the real Jamaican Patois and said, "An if yuh nuh listen, dat mean yuh a wana dem dunca smadi. You hear mi, man!" I will not translate Aunt Lucy's

The Alpha (α)

every word from Jamaican Patois to English. However, what Aunt Lucy was saying was that my opinion counted and that I should not be afraid to express what was on my mind or to voice my concerns regarding any decision. However, if I refused to follow instructions without any justification, then that would imply that I did not care about what she had said or had instructed me to do.

I was amazed by Aunt Lucy's approach to parenting. This was the first time that an adult had told me that my opinion counted and that it was ok to express myself. However, on rare occasions, Aunt Lucy would quote one of her wise proverbs without providing me with further explanation as to why. Nonetheless, she would follow up by saying, "Desmond, I am unable to explain, but just remember, bwoy nuh know everyting wah man know, but man know everyting wah bwoy know because man was once a bwoy." ("A boy does not know everything that a man knows, but a man knows everything that a boy knows because man was once a boy.") (I wonder if Aunt Lucy realized that, according to the scripture, Adam was never a boy.) Her wise phrase can be summed up like this: Not every recommendation or action that is taken in life will be accompanied by an ideal set of explanations or justifications, therefore in these instances, the recipient will just have to trust the messenger. This became even more apparent throughout the times she highlighted the need for me to pursue my academic career even though we both knew that it was not financially feasible.

Because I fully understood her logical approach to life, whenever she recited the "a man knows everything that a boy knows" phrase, I knew not to question her logic beyond that point. Despite the very few times that she

Chapter 3

would use this phrase, her approach to life was very comforting because she was very logical and methodical. For the most part, I was not too taken up by her parenting style because all I had asked of her, and all I was looking forward to receiving from her, was food, clothes, and a roof over my head. In a nutshell, my expectation was pretty much at the first two levels of Maslow's hierarchy of needs.

Aunt Lucy and I would sit and indulge in one-on-one conversations that included school, church, or simply the general aspects of life. This was a colossal difference compared with my former foster mother, with whom just a basic conversation was a chilling experience. For example, when communicating with my former foster mother, I would be thinking about what I would say and how I would say it because I was fully aware of the barrage of insults that would be directed at me if what I said was not grammatically correct. In fact, whenever any of the foster children mispronounced or misused a word, we would most certainly receive a barrage of frightening insults. As for me, it was as though I had to enact an autocorrect proactive measure in my head at all times. What should have been a simple free-flow exchange would turn into the most fearful, heart-pounding, and mindboggling conversation.

My former foster mother's indifference to our opinions extended as far as our attire. Aunt Lucy's approach was at the other end of the spectrum. I remember the first time Aunt Lucy and I went shopping. The moment we walked into the store, I went and stood in a corner waiting for her to do all my shopping. To my surprise, she turned to me and said, "Desmond, what are you doing standing over there! Go and pick out your things, man." After I started

The Alpha (α)

looking around the store for clothing that was not too expensive, Aunt Lucy detected what I was up to and said, "Listen to me man, you do not have to pick out anything that you do not like. Remember, you are the one going to wear them." I could not believe what I was hearing. This was very different, because whenever my former foster mother went shopping, she would deliberately purchase clothes and shoes that were two or three sizes larger than our actual sizes. With Aunt Lucy, I was able to choose my own attire and made sure that everything fit. Nothing like the superman capes George and I had been accustomed to wearing while living with our former foster parents. I remember how worried I was about the overall cost Aunt Lucy was incurring. That was when she turned to me and said, "Don't worry about the money, man! I know that if it is what you want, then I know you are going to take care of it. But if I make you buy things that you don't want, then you are not going to take care of them." In other words, Aunt Lucy was saying that it was in everyone's best interests when I made the decisions regarding my attire.

What was most surprising about our first shopping experience was when Aunt Lucy told me to choose a pair of protective shoes (or water boots as we say in Jamaica). She said, "Desmond, I want yuh fi wear it because I don't want yuh fi cut your foot an catch germs." Aunt Lucy was letting me know that she did not want me to walk about barefooted because of the possibility that sharp objects could pierce or cut my feet and cause me to develop an infection. I know you might be asking what was so special about a pair of protective shoes. Although this might be considered insignificant for most people, for me they were extraordinary gifts when compared to the inhumane

Chapter 3

conditions George and I had been subjected to while living with our former foster parents.

Although I do not know the exact price of a pair of protective shoes in the late 1970s and early 1980s, I do know that providing us with protective footwear was not something that my former foster parents could not afford. Their actions would have given the impression that the costs associated with providing us protective shoes and gloves would have sent them into a financial debt spiral. Even to this day, it still makes my skin crawl to think of how my brother and I were forced to work in those maggot-infested environments, barefooted with many open wounds.

While I am on this topic regarding the love and compassion of Aunt Lucy, let me now fill you in on the happy ending to the severe heartburn (or burn stomach, as per Jamaicans) that I had suffered for over three years while living with my former foster parents. I remember the very first day this heartburn came on me like a heatwave, a volcano, a raging inferno; okay, I do believe I have used enough metaphors to make my point. As the pain radiated through my stomach, I was forced to hunch over because of the severe pain. While I was there hunched over, Aunt Lucy came over and said, "Desmond, what is happening to you, man?" Although it was quite painful for me to speak, I was able to mumble, "Aunt Lucy, my stomach is burning me." Instead of just walking away and brushing it aside as though it were nothing, "Dr. MD" Lucy went into diagnostic mode. She asked, "When did you start feeling this pain, man?" I said, "Long time ago, Aunt Lucy." She probed for a more specific answer, and I told her that I had been experiencing this heartburn for over three years,

The Alpha (α)

but nothing had been done about it. Immediately, and I mean with no hesitation whatsoever, Aunt Lucy said, "Desmond, I am taking you to see the doctor tomorrow morning, yuh hear mi man! We have to go to the doctor tomorrow morning."

Sure enough, the following morning bright and early, Aunt Lucy took me to the doctor. The doctor prescribed some medication (little pink tablets), which provided me with temporary relief. By the way, that was the first time in my life that I remember ever having been taken to a doctor. For the five years I lived with my former foster parents, I was never taken to a doctor once.

When Aunt Lucy noticed that the medication was not ridding me of the annoying stomach problem, she did not just give up and say, "Desmond, I am sorry, but there is nothing else I can do for you." No sir! She did not! One morning after breakfast, Aunt Lucy handed me a glass with some form of liquid and said, "Desmond, I want you to just put this to your head and drink it fast, yuh hear mi man, drink it fast!" I looked into the glass and hesitated. However, Aunt Lucy said, "Desmond, come on, man, drink it for your stomach pain." The minute I heard Aunt Lucy say that it was for my stomach pain, I put the glass to my head and made one big gulp. I thanked her and went to school.

That morning while I was sitting in class, I felt as though a thousand air pockets had erupted in my stomach. Before I could determine what was really going on, I experienced one of the most uncontrollable burps one could ever imagine. A surge of air came gushing out of my mouth like a tornado. The entire class of students, including the instructor, turned their heads and looked at me. Wow! Ladies and gentlemen, that was the loudest and

Chapter 3

most exhaustive burp I had ever had. Not only that, but the severe heartburn subsided significantly. After a couple of treatments from the doctor and Aunt Lucy's homemade remedy, my heartburn went away for a very long time. (For some unknown reason, it resurfaced some twenty-two years later and has been afflicting me on and off ever since, although not as severe as it once was. One mistake that I made, and one that haunts me to this very day, was that I did not ask Aunt Lucy for the list of ingredients she used in her homemade remedy.)

With regards to meals and portion size. Aunt Lucy did not deem it appropriate to give me the leftover scraps. Neither was I being punished whenever I took a snack from the pantry or the refrigerator. I was also welcome to sit at the table and enjoy a meal with the family.

Having fun or providing leisure time was another area in which Aunt Lucy differed from my former foster parents in a significant way. I was surprised when Aunt Lucy told me on several occasions that it was okay for me to participate in the neighborhood activities. She also permitted me to attend the local cricket (not the insect, but a sport similar to baseball) and soccer matches. Aunt Lucy not only told me that I could attend these sporting events, but she reminded me of the upcoming events as well. Although I was grateful to Aunt Lucy for these opportunities, I kept them to a minimum because I was quite busy with my studies and taking care of my vegetable gardens.

Before living with Aunt Lucy, I thought that being a foster child meant that my sole purpose in life was to be someone's helper or yard boy, as I alluded to earlier. I had no idea that my life had any value beyond what my former foster parents, mostly my former foster mother, instilled in me. Although Aunt Lucy taught me otherwise, it was not until I decided to put my life story in writing and had the opportunity to compare and contrast my foster parents, that I truly realized how the compassionate actions of one human being could differ from another in such a profound way. The evidence is undeniably clear that my former foster parents made their fostering decisions solely based on financial gains, while Aunt Lucy's decisions were based on deeply rooted love and compassion. Although Aunt Lucy's worldly possessions were far less than those of my former foster parents, I can say with all surety that she provided me with a lot more, because she gave me hope. I also came to realize that the true art of giving does not originate from the abundance of one's worldly possessions, but instead, from the abundance of one's compassionate soul. This revelation brought tears to my eyes many times.

From a financial perspective, my former foster parents' greed was without conscience. Too much was never enough for them. They had so much but did so little concerning the essential needs of the foster children. Even with their never-ending quest for material possessions and financial gain, in the end they went from having it all to barely having anything at all. Their extreme love for money and the level of arrogance and deceptive behavior they displayed toward the children was undoubtedly the recipe for their downfall. In their later years, the house that had once glowed with elegance and beauty was paled in comparison to what it had been. During one of my visits in their later years, I was saddened by their financial distress and had to reach out to them in such regard. I am not saying this to elevate my self-image or to relish in their downfall, but rather to clarify the point that we should not trade our souls for material gains. The point I am highlighting is this: At no time did Aunt Lucy enact any stringent measures, even though her financial standing was far less than that of my former foster parents.

Finally, I will address briefly Aunt Lucy and my former foster parent's political perspectives. Although I was a child in the early 1980s and my understanding of politics was quite minuscule, I can still recall many of the events that occurred throughout the 1980 election period. This was the case because this election cycle brought so much bloodshed, death, destruction of property, and food *shortages*, which eventually led to food rationing and food marriages and many other instabilities that swept across the island.[5] Notice that I emphasized the word shortages because that further depleted the little food our foster parents were providing us. Even at one point, we had no sugar to sweeten our tea and beverages. So, as you can tell, I was certainly not a fan of this election. Okay, I think I need to stop reminiscing on spilt sugar.

In addition to the excessive violence and the food shortages, I remember this election because my former foster parents were out and about canvassing the district. Their objective was to convince everyone to vote for the Jamaica Labour Party (JLP), which was headed by Edward Seaga. I overheard them saying that if the People's National Party (PNP) were to win the election then they were going to be forced to share their

---

[5] Food marriages occurred when customers were forced to purchase other goods that they may or may not have needed. For example, throughout such times, if you needed a pound of rice, then you had to purchase a bar or two of washing soap or some other slow-turnover or least-desirable item.

The Alpha (α)

possessions because Michael Manley (leader of the PNP) was a socialist. My first reaction was, yes, let us all vote for the PNP so that my foster parents would be forced to share their meals with me. Okay, no such thought crossed my mind at the time, but I simply could not resist being witty. Anyway, with my limited knowledge of politics, I had no clue what they were saying, so that was where my political understanding ended as it relates to my former foster parents.

However, several years later, while living with Aunt Lucy, I happened to recognize a nicely framed portrait of Michael Manley displayed in her living room. I was a bit curious as to why Aunt Lucy would want to cherish a picture of a "socialist" leader. With that in mind, I asked her if she knew that Manley's philosophy was to take away half of what she owned and give it to poor people. To my surprise, she told me that Manley was a good man because he looked out for the poor and the disenfranchised, and had it not been for his programs the residents of Sawyers community would not have had access to clean water. She told me that when Manley had visited the district and heard that the residents were drinking water from a pond that was contaminated with cow feces and other harmful bacteria, he immediately enacted a program to build water catchment facilities in the homes of the residents who had land space; and for those who did not own homes or did not have the land space, public water catchment facilities were built strategically throughout the district. She told me that it was through this program that she had obtained her water tank. Finally, she told me that this was a program that had been implemented throughout other districts as well.

Chapter 3

I was astonished to have heard such a profound contrast with respect to two different individuals' political viewpoints, even though they both shared the same religious point of view. However, as I ponder over this experience, I realize that people have different political points of view that are based on their views of the world and how they perceive their fellow humankind. My former foster parents were quick to use the political system to justify their actions and to safeguard their interests. Not to mention that a significant portion of their wealth was derived through ill-gotten gains. In other words, much of their wealth had been accrued through the exploitation of the lives and well-being of the foster children and the Child Development System. However, Aunt Lucy did not have the same mindset with respect to lending a helping hand to a disenfranchised person like me. This is just a preview but as you continue to traverse my life story you will realize that colossal difference between my current and former foster parents.

Rebuilding the Foundation of Life

After Aunt Lucy and I had established a level of understanding, it was time to move forward and commence living my life anew. This decree was not only a matter of "so has it been said," but it was also a matter of "so shall it be done." She signaled to me to take up my bag and follow her, and, without any hesitation, I did so. She opened a door and told me that this would be my room.

The minute I walked through the door, she said, "Desmond, do you see the room and the condition it is in?" I replied, "Yes, Aunt Lucy." She then said, "I want it to be this way at all times, do you hear mi, man?" Once

The Alpha (α)

again, I said, "Yes, Aunt Lucy." If keeping my room clean was all I had to worry about, then this would certainly be an easy task, especially compared to the amount of cleaning I had to do while living with my former foster parents. Aunt Lucy then told me to put my clothes in the closet and relax for a while. It took me less than five minutes to put away my belongings, because my entire life's possession was less than what could fit in carry-on luggage. After I was through, I sat at the foot of the bed and relaxed for a while. I am not sure why I needed to relax. Probably I was quite exhausted from all that work putting away my wardrobe. Okay, here is the truth: I was overwhelmed with what had just transpired and needed to sit down while I came to terms with reality. Not only did I have a roof over my head, but I also had a room exclusively to myself.

Those were all the instructions Aunt Lucy conveyed because she had to return to the shop and tend to her customers. Just to recap, Aunt Lucy operated a little grocery shop that was attached to the front of the house. The shop was in full operation throughout her younger years, however, she had scaled back the operation significantly. She now sold a limited assortment of animal feed, snacks, and few dozens of bottled beverages.

Later that morning, Aunt Lucy informed her cousin, Sister Lin, that I was now a member of the family. Sister Lin and I were no strangers, as she was a member of the Hope Gospel Hall and worked briefly as a live-in helper for my former foster parents. How could I ever forget Sister Lin, when she used to provide us with some of the best sweet potato puddings.

At around noon Aunt Lucy presented me with lunch. I was not looking forward to any lunch because I had not

Chapter 3

been accustomed to having three meals per day while living with Ms. Clemmie. After lunch, I met several of the Hope Gospel Hall church members and they were all excited to see me. Later that afternoon, I noticed that Aunt Lucy was very busy preparing dinner and tending to her customers. I wanted to give her a helping hand, but I was not yet familiar with the operation, so I decided to stay out of her way until I learned the process.

Here is an insight into the operation of a typical Jamaican grocery shop, at least the ones in the rural areas. First, the owner or operator did not put price labels on the products. Second, forget about scanning the barcode of a product at a point of sale (POS) system because there weren't any. Instead, the prices were stored away in the shopkeeper's head. Therefore, it would be difficult if not impossible for anyone to assist such a person without prior knowledge. With this lack of information, the customer would have to ask the shopkeeper, "A humuch fi dat?" ("How much for that?") If the prices were not what was expected, the customer would raise his or her voice, saying, "Den a sumuch fi dat?" ("Does it really cost that much?" Or, "Why is that particular item so expensive?") Anyway, that is all I have for now regarding Jamaican shop keeping 101.

That evening Aunt Lucy provided me with a very delicious dinner. Aunt Lucy also allowed me to sit at the dining table; she did not ask me to take my meal and sit outside or someplace on the floor. Once again, it was a wonderful experience to find myself seated at the table and not on the floor or outside on a little wooden bench surrounded by greedy pets. After dinner, I spent some time with Aunt Lucy in the shop and observed as she

The Alpha (α)

Aunt Lucy's home. This was once my home sweet home.

served and conversed with her customers. I also learned a little more regarding her business method. I was not a total stranger to the shopkeeping operation because I had operated my former foster parents' grocery shop. However, Aunt Lucy managed her grocery shop more like a social gathering because she barely had anything in the shop. In fact, most of her customers would come by just to sit and talk. That evening Aunt Lucy kept the shop open until approximately 9:00 p.m., which was the norm for her Saturday evening hours. After the customers went home, Aunt Lucy and I closed up the shop and retired to bed.

Every time that I found myself going through a dramatic transformation, I would find it difficult to sleep the first couple of nights. Sure enough, this was one of those times. That night I was so overwhelmed with joy to the

Chapter 3

point that I found myself reminiscing about my life and how the dark clouds that had been looming over me were a thing of the past. Despite the overwhelming emotions, I managed to get a nap in the early hours of the morning.

I woke up at the break of dawn. To my surprise, Aunt Lucy was already out of bed and in the kitchen preparing breakfast. I went into the kitchen and greeted her with a big and pleasant, "Good morning, Aunt Lucy," and she replied likewise. She followed up by saying, "Desmond, come and eat your breakfast and get ready for Sunday school." I ate breakfast, took a shower, dressed, and went to church. I was a bit early, so I sat in the church hall and listened to Pastor Sommers as he led the early morning devotion.

Over the years, Pastor Sommers taught me a wealth of guiding principles that helped to shape my everyday decisions. At first, it appeared as though Pastor Sommers and my father's religious doctrine and practices were in stark contrast with each other. However, after closer examination, I come to realize that they have a lot more in common as it relates to their beliefs and philosophy. Both were committed and seemed to have a deep abiding faith with respect to their religious beliefs. My father paid homage to Jah through the reading of the Bible (not sure what version), chants, and meditations, while Pastor Sommers paid homage to God through praying, preaching, teaching, singing, and reading of the King James version of the Bible. My father believed strongly that smoking marijuana, meditation, and chanting were noble forms of worship that should be devoted unto Jah, while Pastor Sommers believed that smoking should not be used as a form of worship ritual. In this context, the Rastafarian culture could be referred to as a sect of Christianity. I am quite sure that a person without prior knowledge of the Rastafarian and Christian doctrines most likely would experience difficulty rationalizing which one to choose. I have experienced both and have chosen to adopt the Christian faith. However, had I not been removed from my father's care, then I would most likely embrace the Rastafarian doctrine.

    Back to the moment at hand. Later that morning, the other children started arriving for the 10:00 a.m. Sunday school ritual. All of the church members, including the Sunday school teachers and the children, were very happy to see me. They were also quite curious and wanted to know where I was living. They were surprised when I told them that I was living with Aunt Lucy. After the Sunday school program ended, I stayed behind with a number of the children for the 11:00 to 12:00 church service. I was no stranger to the routine because I had been attending Hope Gospel Hall for the past five years

    Just before the commencement of the 11:00 a.m. service, my former foster parents came into the building. I am not sure if they had noticed that I was also present. However, after the morning service, they saw me conversing with the church members. They also noticed that the church members were delighted to see me and to know that Aunt Lucy had taken me into her home. I clearly could see that my former foster parents were not happy at all. They did not greet me with open arms because they were not in agreement with Aunt Lucy's decision. In fact, Aunt Lucy told me that when my former foster parents heard that she (Aunt Lucy) was about to foster me, they came to her and not only tried to convince her but

Chapter 3

demanded that she not follow through on her decision. They even went as far as to let her know that I was a thief and a gambler and that she was making a big mistake and would regret her decision.

I am not sure why my former foster parents would try to convince Aunt Lucy that I was a thief and that I had gambled away hundreds of dollars. I really thought that they would have realized by now that no rational human being would ever believe such baseless fabrication. Moreover, Ms. Davis had already confronted them in such regard. The first time I could see why they resorted to such a made-up accusation was because they did not think that Ms. Davis would put the onus on them to justify their claim. However, after approximately a month one would think that my former foster parents would not have resorted to such a claim after having ample time to think about what they were really saying. This type of behavior is beyond my comprehension. I am baffled as to what was going on in their minds as to why they think that Aunt Lucy would not have had the same reaction Ms. Davis had. In the current context, their claim would be equivalent to your child who is less than sixteen years old stealing thousands of dollars from your possession and you just sit back and do nothing about it for many years.

However, I should not be shocked because after abusing Jacqueline to the point that she had welt marks, cuts, and bruises over her body, my former foster mother stood there with a straight face trying to convince me that Jacqueline was not speaking the truth when my brother and I were abused in like manner. Even Maxwell who was a boarder, not a foster child, was also abused. If the Child Development Agency had done their due diligence, then my foster parents would have a lot of explaining as to why the foster children had so many welt marks, cuts, bruises, and open wounds all over their bodies. Unfortunately, this is the typical behavior people display when insanity becomes their norm.

When Aunt Lucy did not heed their demands, they became quite resentful toward her. Not only that, but they withdrew their membership from Hope Gospel Hall shortly thereafter. I am not sure if it was based solely on Aunt Lucy's decision to foster me against their will or if it was for other reasons. One thing I know for sure is that my former foster parents did not take it lightly when their authority was challenged.

Irrespective of the reason or reasons, I knew that my former foster parents were determined to prove that I was not deserving of anything good in life. The message they were conveying to Aunt Lucy was that whenever they had rendered a person's (Desmond's) life insignificant, how dare you (Aunt Lucy) challenge their authority? Rendering a person's life as insignificant was exactly what they had done to my only brother when they persuaded the CDA that he was not deserving of a foster parent. In the end, they personally took George to a juvenile correctional institution for no apparent reason other than that he spoke out against their injustice and would no longer tolerate their inhumane treatment.

My former foster parents had significant financial influence over the church, not to mention their desire to be treated as exceptional. However, I am very grateful to God that they did not have any personal, political or economic influence over Aunt Lucy. If that had been the case, then they would certainly have exercised such leverage,

Chapter 3

and Aunt Lucy would have been forced to accept their demands concerning me. Even though they withdrew their membership from the church, that did not constitute the end to the existence of the church. Although my former foster parents' desire was to destroy my life, I was confident that time would eventually heal all wounds.

Okay, let move on and see how the rest of the day's activities transpired. After the conclusion of the morning service and the short meet and greet, we dispersed to our homes. Aunt Lucy and Sister Lin prepared dinner and we all, except Sister Lin, sat around the dining-room table and enjoyed our Sunday meal. Sister Lin was always welcome at the table, but most of the time, she found it quite comforting to sit in the kitchen and enjoy her meals. I guess she wanted to be close to the pot so that she could have easy access to a second helping. Not really. Anyway, she spent most of her time in the kitchen because she was always blending her special drink or baking her favorite sweet potato pudding. Her homemade chocolate and her tasty sweet potato puddings were the best! The flavors are still lighting up my taste buds even to this very day. However, if you asked her for the recipe or instructions of how she went about baking her favorite sweet potato pudding, she would respond, "Hell at the top, hell at the bottom, and Hallelujah in the middle." Actually, she was describing a conventional oven.

After we were through with dinner, Aunt Lucy went to her room for a little nap and Sister Lin and I had a long chat while she washed the dishes and cleaned the kitchen. That day, most of our conversation was centered around when and why I was removed from my former foster parents' home. Later that evening, we got dressed and went

The Alpha (α)

to church for the Sunday night service, which commenced at 7:00 p.m. and lasted until 9:00 p.m. After the conclusion of the night service, we went home, enjoyed a light snack, and finally retired to bed. These activities constituted the first full day of life with Aunt Lucy.

The next morning, Monday, I got up quite early but, once again, Aunt Lucy was already in the kitchen preparing breakfast. As soon as I sat down to eat, Aunt Lucy pulled up a chair, and said, "Desmond, I want you to go to school. Yuh hear mi, man? I want yuh to go to school! I am going to speak to Mr. Golding so that you can start school next week. Do you hear mi, man?"

I remember answering her with a reluctant, "Yes, Aunt Lucy." Although I was happy, I was a bit hesitant with my reply because I knew that this undertaking would impose a financial strain on her limited resources. Nevertheless, upon hearing my yes response, Aunt Lucy concluded the conversation, as it pertained to school. After breakfast, I assisted Aunt Lucy and Sister Lin with their chores.

Later that afternoon, Aunt Lucy told me not to wait on her to serve lunch because I was free to take whatever I wanted. Wow! Another startling difference compared to my former foster parents. While living with them, my brother and I dared not take a snack, drink, or a cool drink of water from the refrigerator. In fact, she would punch us repeatedly on our arms whenever she caught us taking anything from the cupboard or the refrigerator. However, Aunt Lucy did not give me a reason to fear being punched or slapped. With that in mind, I fixed myself a sandwich and washed it down with a cold drink.

Later that evening, I ate dinner then I spent the rest of the evening with Aunt Lucy in the shop, indulging in chitchat while she attended to her customers. At approximately 8:00 p.m., Aunt Lucy closed the shop, and we retired to bed. Tuesday was just about the same as Monday except that, at approximately 6:00 p.m., I accompanied Aunt Lucy and Sister Lin to one of the church member's homes for the Tuesday night women's gathering. Seeing that this was a women's gathering, I had to sit and be quiet for the entire duration. This was the time when the women were in charge, and even if a male figure like me happened to be around, he was not allowed to speak or take part in any of the activities.

The real question is why I had been allowed to attend the women's meeting in the first place. Was it because I had once worn a pair of female shoes? Okay, that was simply not the case. I did so because there was nothing else for me to do at home. However, for all you male readers out there, please come a little closer because I am about to reveal a little secret of what goes on at a women's gathering. First, this is the time when the women would get together and discuss how disgusting the men are and how it was a wonderful experience to be away from them. Just kidding! Here is the truth and nothing but the truth. This is the time when the women would discuss their role in the church and ways in which they could bond together and support each other. After attending a number of the women's meetings, it caused me to wonder why there was never a men's meeting where we could get together and discuss similar issues. I guess guys do not need other guys looking out for them because it is "Every man for himself." Anyway, the women's meeting lasted approximately two hours, after which the women indulged in a little "off-the-record" chitchat

The Alpha (α)

for a couple of minutes before dispersing to their respective homes. Finally, Aunt Lucy, Sister Lin and I had a tasty treat before retiring to bed.

Wednesday was pretty much the same as Tuesday, except that Wednesday was a prayer meeting night. After dinner, we showered, dressed, and went to church for the prayer meeting. We had a big turnout for this occasion because it was considered the most important weekday gathering. The event started with the singing of songs and reading of scripture verses from the Bible. At the end of the first segment, the church members divided into two groups. One group consisted of the church brothers and the other the church sisters. The brothers went into one of the back rooms, while the sisters stayed in the church hall. We took turns and prayed; giving God thanks and much appreciation for salvation, mercies, grace, blessings, and just about anything that was near and dear to our hearts. If a brother or a sister were ill, going through difficulties, or personal issues, then the pastor would ask us to remember such an individual in our prayers. I am not sure what I prayed for that day, but I am quite sure that I had more than enough to be thankful for.

Thursday was pretty much the same as the other weekdays except that no church events were scheduled for that day. Friday was my favorite weekday because I always looked forward to attending the young people's meeting. After completing my Friday chores, I ate dinner, showered, dressed, and went to church for the meeting, which commenced at 7:00 p.m. and lasted anywhere from two to two and a half hours, depending on the program. It reminded me of game nights when people (mostly young people) would come together to have fun.

Chapter 3

A typical young people's meeting program would be contingent upon the time of the year and the religious rituals. For example, throughout the Christmas and Easter seasons, we reenacted bible stories and celebrated other religious rituals associated with Christ's birth and crucifixion, respectively. On a typical Friday, we would break into groups and challenge each other through Bible drills and other competitive games. Brother Victor and Pastor Sommers were the architects of the young people's meeting. Over the years, they dedicated much of their time and resources to this cause, while at the same time helping us to understand the Bible and our faith in the Lord.

What did Aunt Lucy do on a typical Friday evening? She would keep the shop open until around 10:00 p.m. Several of the church members and other residents from the community would stop by and have a couple of drinks and play dominoes or just sit around and talk, mostly telling stories. Whenever I was among them, most of their stories would be centered on their childhoods. They would start out by saying, "Unnu young bwoy nuh . . . , because when we a weh bwoy . . ." ("You young boys do not know . . . , because when we were boys . . .") My takeaway from their conversation was this: The younger generation simply does not appreciate the real value of life because we tend to take everything for granted. In other words, what the current generation is enjoying today, they tend to forget that someone did the hard work to make it possible. I must confess that, at times, I find myself taking for granted the hard work of others, and in this instance, I do concur with their philosophy.

Saturday morning I assisted Aunt Lucy and Sister Lin with the farming chores. Later, I went to the grocery

The Alpha (α)

store and purchased the week's groceries. Although Aunt Lucy operated a grocery shop, she did not sell any meat or produce. Therefore, I would have to purchase those items from Mr. McKoy's grocery store, which was located approximately one mile away. I also went into the nearby bushes in search of dried wood for fuel. This was necessary because, due to financial constraints, we needed another fuel source so as minimize our propane costs. In the evening, I cleaned the refrigerator, followed by my room, and that completed one full week living with Aunt Lucy.

I will not repeat each week's activities; instead, I will fast-forward to the major events. The following Saturday was special because Aunt Lucy and I went shopping for my back-to-school uniform and accessories. I remember this shopping experience quite well. It started out when Aunt Lucy and I journeyed to Brown's Town (Brown's Town is a little district that is located in the parish of St Ann) shopping center and open market. Upon arrival, we went to one of the apparel stores. Aunt Lucy told me to choose my crepes and uniforms, along with underwear, socks, shorts, rags, handkerchiefs, a belt, and other accessories. She allowed me to choose my own uniform and make sure that everything fits properly. Wow! This was a colossal difference in parenting and one that is hard for me to explain with words.

Finally, Back in School

Bright and early Monday morning, I got up but, once again, never early enough because Aunt Lucy was already in the kitchen preparing breakfast. The minute I walked into the dining room, she greeted me, "Desmond, eat yuh

Chapter 3

food an get ready fi school because Mr. Golding expecting to see yuh today." (Desmond, eat your breakfast and get ready for school because Mr. Golding is expecting to see you today). With much enthusiasm, I ate my breakfast, showered, dressed, and walked approximately one mile to school with the other children from the neighborhood. Once again, I was very fortunate that I was not wearing a pair of female shoes, because it would undoubtedly have been a very painful walk. You should have been there to see me sporting my new school uniform and my new pair of sneakers. Not only that, but I had pearly white teeth and clean underwear because there was no longer a shortage of basic necessities. It was awesome! Okay, a little too much detail but I just could not help myself, especially when I reflect on the vast difference between foster parents.

Although I only had six months to complete my ninth-grade academic career at the all-age academic level, I was still very happy to be given such a wonderful opportunity.[6] As soon as I arrived, the principal, Talbert Golding, greeted me. Wasting no time, he beckoned to me to accompany him to his office so that we could finalize the registration process. Not only was Mr. Golding the school principal, but he was my ninth-grade teacher as well. This arrangement meant that I would be seeing a lot of the principal throughout the six-month academic period. At the time, I was not sure if having the principal as my teacher was in my best interest. However, it turned out to be an advantage because Mr. Golding was a very kind and

---

6 By the way, the all-age school in Jamaica exceeds a US middle school by one grade level. This was the eighth grade for the USA and the ninth grade for Jamaica.

The Alpha (α)

Sawyers All-Age School is where I completed the final six months of my 9th grade academic year in 1984. Picture 2009

Sawyers All-Age School is where I completed the final six months of my 9th grade academic year in 1984. Picture 2019

respectable person who cared deeply about the well-being of the students. I was also very fortunate that my former foster mother was not teaching at the school. If she had been, then she would most certainly have shown up while my class was in session and demanded that Mr. Golding dish out physical punishment (beating) on me.

The major downside was the fact that I was about to complete the ninth grade with more like a third- or fourth-grade education. I was definitely not smarter than a fifth-grader. Therefore, it was quite clear that I had a lot of catching up to do. However, the minute I sneezed, and before someone could say, "Bless you," the six months went by and it was graduation day. I graduated from the Sawyers All-Age School in June of 1984. I was delighted to have finally completed the ninth-grade requirements and earned my first academic certification. When reflecting on moments like this, I realized that had my brother not been deprived of his human dignity, this would most certainly have been his accomplishment as well.

Although my academic standing was far below the level required to attend high school, this limitation did not signify the end of my academic career. In fact, there were secondary and tertiary level academic paths that were made available for children such as myself who were not fortunate to attend high school. Not having the financial resources was a major hurdle for parents, such as Aunt Lucy, who were struggling to make ends meet. Although I would have liked to further my academic career, I knew that it was not financially feasible. With no further schooling in my prospects, I was at home helping Aunt Lucy and Sister Lin with the farming and household chores. As the summer holiday was coming to an end,

The Alpha (α)

I was contemplating the idea of expanding the farm so that we could make a little money to provide for our basic needs. However, Aunt Lucy intervened and put the brakes on my farm-expansion plan rather quickly.

One bright and early morning while I was having breakfast, Aunt Lucy pulled up a chair, sat beside me, and, in a somewhat stern but informative voice, said, "Desmond, we need to talk!" Immediately I thought that I had done something wrong and was about to receive a verbal scolding. To my surprise, Aunt Lucy was about to have another conversation with me regarding my academic career. She said, "Desmond, this is a farming village, and everyone around here does farming for a living, but I am not going to let that be your first choice. Do you hear mi, man? I want your first choice to be school. So on Monday morning we are going to go to Albert Town and try and get you into school. Do you hear mi, man?"

Aunt Lucy was not anti-farming, but she realized that acquiring a good education was the only way for me to exercise my true potential. Not only that, but in the district of Sawyers, farming is done in a labor-intensive manner due to the rugged terrain and the lack of proper farming equipment. Therefore, the average farmer works many long and tiring hours but does not produce much.

I was overwhelmed with joy. However, I was very much concerned knowing that Aunt Lucy was going out of her way to provide me with far more than the basic food, clothes, and shelter I had asked of her. I also knew that this ambitious proposal would put a severe strain on her meager financial resources. Despite my reservations, Aunt Lucy said, "Desmond, you don't worry about a ting, you hear me, man. You just leave it in the hands of the

Chapter 3

Lord. You hear mi, man? Just leave it in the hands of the Lord." She went on to say, "Desmond, all you need to have is the desire."

I realized that Aunt Lucy was not speaking from an economic perspective, but instead from a compassionate, heartfelt desire. And that was when I replied with an enthusiastic, "Yes, Aunt Lucy, I want to go to school!" Although I had serious reservations regarding the associated costs, I was very happy for the opportunity to further my academic career. My assurance was all Aunt Lucy needed to put the process in motion. In this situation, I believe that Aunt Lucy's compassion led her to think and act in ways that were outside the realm of her known capabilities. This is why I am fully convinced that economic feasibility is always in stark contrast with the *will* of a person to succeed. In other words, financial feasibility should not be used to hinder the *desire* of a person, system, or nation to succeed

The following Monday morning, Aunt Lucy and I boarded a bus to Albert Town, Trelawny. This town was approximately eight miles from Sawyers and hosted one of the secondary vocational schools that accommodated children between twelve and seventeen years old, enrolled in the seventh through the eleventh grades. This academic institution was the ideal choice for a person like me, who did not have the financial and academic standing necessary to attend any of the prominent high schools located throughout the island. So once again, I was traveling with *confidence* and was on my way to charter a new academic course.

After making many stops, the bus finally arrived at Albert Town. Aunt Lucy and I got off at the town square and walked a little distance to where the school was located. The compound was peacefully quiet because the students were out for the summer break. Just before we entered the administrative building, we were greeted by one of the staff members who inquired about the reason for our visit. Aunt Lucy told her that she was there to sign me up for school. The staff member said, "Mam, I am sorry, but we are fully booked for the upcoming school year, and you need to try another school or come back next year." However, Aunt Lucy would not take no for an answer. She pleaded my case to the woman. She said, "Please, there is no way I can have him out of school for a whole year. That is just too much time for him to be out of school and you know that young people will get into trouble when they have nothing to do." After a lot of persuading and pleading, the woman finally heeded Aunt Lucy's plea. Probably she did not want to disappoint a parent who cared passionately about her child's academic career.

The second hurdle came when the administrative staff member informed us that in order for me to be accepted to the school, I had to sit an entrance test. With that said, she told me to follow her to the administration building. She took me to a conference room and said, "Please have a seat, I will be right back." Within a couple of minutes, she returned with the entrance test and handed it to me. After I was through with the test, she took it and graded it right there. She stepped out of the room in a hurry, without letting me know if I had been successful or not. The last thing I wanted was a repeat of what had happened when my former foster mother discovered that I was unable to read or write. Or the disappointment I went

Chapter 3

through when I found out that I had failed the high school entrance exam.

Nonetheless I followed her, but from a distance, because I thought that I had done poorly on the test and that she was about to give my foster mother an earful for bringing a dummy with the lowest IQ on the property. Even to this very day, I am still unable to remember what happened between the time I took the entrance test from her and the time I handed it back to her. Everything was a blur. So there I was lagging approximately fifteen feet behind, looking on as she walked briskly toward my foster mother. To my surprise, she said, "Mam, based on Desmond's test results, he definitely belongs in school. Not only did he acquire a passing grade, but his score met the 10-1 level requirement." The woman went on to say, "Although 10-1 is completely booked, I have no other choice but to place him in this section because if I placed him in any of the other sections it would be a setback for him." She turned to me and said, "Congratulations! See you in September." Wow! That was undoubtedly a miracle because, even to this very day, I am still unable to recall any of the questions that were on the test. This outcome was beyond my human comprehension but, once again, I have come to realize and acknowledge that with God, all things are possible.

At the time, I had no idea what she meant by the 10-1 level requirement. Later I found out that the tenth and eleventh grades were divvied up into three sections each. That is, 10-1, 10-2, 10-3, 11-1, 11-2, and 11-3, with 10-1 and 11-1 hosting the students who had done exceptionally well on the entrance test or their ninth- and tenth-grade final exams. The remainder of the students were placed in

The Alpha (α)

10-2, 10-3, 11-2, and 11-3, accordingly. From my perspective, it was considered more than an honor to be placed in the 10-1 grade level. I could see the radiant joy beaming from Aunt Lucy's face. Her expression of happiness said it all. As for me, there are no words to express the way I felt that day. Aunt Lucy and I expressed our sincere gratitude to the lady, then we commenced our journey back home.

While at home, I spent the rest of the summer performing routine chores such as taking care of the farm and, occasionally, giving Aunt Lucy a helping hand with the operation of the shop. After I was through with my chores, I played a couple of games on my Xbox, then my PlayStation, and finally my Nintendo Wii. Okay, please ignore every word in the previous statement because there was absolutely no such entertainment system in the home, not even a television. If you consider a radio to be an entertainment system, then Aunt Lucy did have a very old radio that sounded like raindrops pouring down on a tin roof. Anyway, after a long day at home, I was very eager to go to church. (Probably if we took away these mega entertainment gadgets from our children, then they might be more inclined to attend church. Please consider my suggestion to be just a thought because we know that such an action would trigger an all-out rebellion.) The long summer finally ended, and it was time for me to cross a new and exciting educational frontier.

The Unexpected Appearance

There I was, waiting with much anticipation for the day to come when I could finally embark on yet another educational journey. However, out of nowhere, my only brother,

Chapter 3

whom I had not seen in over three years, somewhat magically appeared. In fact, I had not seen George since the day our former foster parents had removed him from their home and dropped him off at the juvenile correctional institution for boys. Over those years I always look forward to his return. However, after a while my hope of ever seeing my brother again started to diminish. At first, I did not recognize him because he was sporting nappy hair and looked quite different from the brother I once knew. However, I recognized him when he got closer. We greeted each other and he told me that he had gone to our former foster parents' house to remove me from their care, but they had told him that I was no longer living with them, but instead, was living with Aunt Lucy in Sawyers. He continued by letting me know that I was living in Babylon and that I should leave immediately and come back home to live with him and our father in Zion. He also emphasized the need for me to come back home where I could be free to smoke marijuana and meditate on Jah. His exact words were, "Come home, Iah, an mek wi bun di chillum, meditate an give tanks to Jah." ("Come home, my brother, so that we can smoke marijuana from the chillum, meditate, and give thanks unto Jah.")

Based on his initial conversation, I knew that my brother had once again been indoctrinated into our father's Rastafarian philosophy. I was no stranger to the Rastafarian lifestyle and the psychological struggles we had endured throughout our childhood. However, Aunt Lucy's overwhelming compassion had taught me that not all foster parents are like my former foster parents and that there are people who really care. At no time did Aunt Lucy made me feel like I was less of a person or that my sole purpose in

The Alpha (α)

life was to become someone's property. Looking back, if my brother had visited me while I was living with my former foster parents, I probably would have heeded his advice.

As I stood there and listened to George explain why it was important for me to come back home, I was saddened and deeply troubled when he outlined his many reasons, which included the harsh and inhumane treatment that we had been subjected to while living with our former foster parents. He also informed me of the physical and psychological abuse he had endured while living at Copse, the juvenile correctional institution. He went on to say that life at Copse had reached a point that he simply could not take it anymore and, eventually, he had run away in search of a better life. He told me that he had walked for many miles, day and night through the woods so as elude the authorities, until he eventually found our father's home. My brother was speaking the truth because I did a bit of research and found out that Copse was indeed a very horrible place, as noted by a reporter from the *Jamaica Observer's* Western Bureau (Williams 2005).

At one point in our conversation, Aunt Lucy intervened and tried to have a rational conversation with my brother but he could not be persuaded. My brother had lost trust in everyone except our father. Most likely, this was attributable to his traumatic childhood experiences and the fact that he was deeply rooted in our father's Rastafarian doctrine. In the end, Aunt Lucy had no other choice but to let George know that I would not be accompanying him back to our father's home.

I do not have any odds with the Rastafarian culture or doctrine; however, what I do know is that my father practiced a form of Rastafarianism that was at odds with

Chapter 3

societal norms. Why would my father have chosen to have his children removed from his care just to preserve his philosophy? Could it be that my father had gone through experiences similar to those my brother had gone through? Unfortunately, I never had an opportunity to converse with my father in such a manner. Therefore, I do not know what could have caused him to resort to such a deeply rooted doctrine.

After having some time to reflect on my brother's life, including this incident, I realized that my brother was not really trying to brainwash me. Instead, he cared deeply about my well-being. My brother was trying to remove me from a system that had failed him in every way imaginable. I believe that we should use moments such as this to reflect on our lives and to make sure that our actions do not bring about harm to the less fortunate, especially those children who have been placed in our care or subjected to our jurisdiction.

My former foster parents were the ones who physically and psychologically abused my brother. However, it was our former foster mother who humiliated him by addressing him as a dog and scavenger. On many occasions, she told him that he was not going to come to anything good in life. She went as far as to let him know that he was going to live and die like a dog. And in the end, she made sure that he was taken to a place where it was virtually impossible for him to have a chance at a normal life. I could only imagine what was going through my former foster parents' (more so my foster mother's) mind that day when they saw my brother. I wonder if they had any remorse, or if they were satisfied and considered their actions as "mission accomplished."

The Alpha (α)

My heart goes out to my only brother because he suffered so much physical and mental abuse as a child. My brother experienced a miserable life in what our father described as the Babylonian system. Our foster parents were the ones who had been entrusted to provide us a better life. They were the ones who had promised to help us realize the difference between a normal life and that of our father's Rastafarian doctrine, our mother's poverty-stricken life, and an orphanage where only our basic needs were met. However, they have failed and are the primary reason why my brother despised those who professed Christianity.

I am quite sure that my father did not have to do much to convince my brother that his Rastafarian doctrine was the more noble choice. Neither did he have to do much to convince my brother that the Babylonian system is evil, that those who profess Christianity are corrupt, and that those with economic and social influence use such power to oppress the innocent through coercive and deceptive tactics. Our foster parents' actions validated our father's assertions that all Christians are hypocrites and that the systems of this world should not be trusted. Therefore, how could anyone fault my brother for rejecting the version of Christianity that our former foster parents were conveying?

This was yet another very sad and painful day for me, to watch as George turned his back and walked away from the very people who could have helped him and who wanted to help him. I felt as though my brother and I were in two different worlds. The most painful outcome of this unforgettable occurrence was the fact that my brother and I were so close physically, but mentally and philosophically we were so far apart.

Chapter 3

I can only reminisce on the days my brother and I spent with our foster parents; how my brother would work very hard (both physically and academically) to prove himself but, instead of receiving a little acknowledgment, he was humiliated every time. I am quite sure that if George had been given the opportunity, he would have lived out his life's dream of becoming a proud and resourceful member of society. Instead, he spent his entire life searching for an identity; searching for someone or something to fill the emptiness he felt deep within his soul. In the end, he surrendered his life to drugs and alcohol. Just like everyone else around him, I was unable to hear his cry. Neither did I understand his life beyond his physical appearance or the magnitude of his psychological struggle. Eventually, he found himself living on the streets with absolutely no hope of ever seeing a brighter tomorrow. It took many years and a traumatic life encounter for me to understand just a sliver of the psychological pain my brother had endured his entire life.

A visit that was intended to bring us closer together as brothers did just the opposite. And that was the last contact I had with my brother until approximately nine years later when we crossed paths once more. (Our second reunion is outlined in volume 4.) Even to this very day, I am still saddened and heartbroken to have witnessed what had become of my only brother. I can assure you that from the very day my former foster parents took my brother away from me, it left an emptiness that I feel deep within my soul. Although my brother and I were separated, I never stop thinking about him. The mere fact that he came searching for me was a vivid reminder that he had not forgotten about me either.

The Alpha (α)

In Search of Higher Education

The final weekend before school commenced, Aunt Lucy and I went on another back-to-school shopping spree. My school attire included two pairs of khaki pants, three khaki shirts, and a pair of shoes. Just to clarify, my footwear was not crepe or sneakers and most certainly not a pair of female shoes! Instead, it was a pair of Viking dress shoes. Once again, Aunt Lucy allowed me to choose my own uniform. Her only input had to do with the choice of footwear. She told me to choose a pair of formal shoes and several pairs of dress socks instead of sneakers and gym socks, because she wanted me to look very professional. After choosing my uniform and shoes, I tried them on to make sure that they fit properly. Once again, this was quite unusual for me. After purchasing my uniform and other accessories, I finalized my shopping with the purchase of a backpack, notebooks, pens, and pencils. Wow! With this many resources, one would think that I was about to enroll at a prestigious college such as Harvard or Princeton. Well, knowing me, it would be more like MIT. Or seeing that it was Jamaica, it would have been the College of Arts, Science and Technology (CAST), today is known as the University of Technology, Jamaica (UTech, Ja.).

Due to the extra activities, the weekend flew by rather quickly. Monday morning, I got up very early, but once again, Aunt Lucy was up and busy in the kitchen. It was quite obvious that she was the queen of the early rise. Seeing that I did not have to prepare my own breakfast, I showered, dressed, and went straight to the dining room where my meal was nicely laid out on the table. While I was eating, Aunt Lucy sat beside me and gave

Chapter 3

me a little "how important education is" pep talk. After I was through eating, she went into the little grocery shop, took out $15, gave it to me, and said, "Desmond, this $15 is for the week. It is for your lunch and bus fare." Why $15 a week? Well, Aunt Lucy must have done the math because I had no idea how much it cost to attend a secondary institution.

After receiving my weekly allowance, I went by the roadway and waited for the bus. Before I could make myself comfortable, I heard the Confidence bus horn echoing through the mountains. The driver was signaling to the passengers or *potential passengers* to get to the roadway before he got there. You might be wondering why I emphasized the words potential passengers in the above statement. Well, if you are a bit curious, then here is the reason. If you had a need to travel and were not by the roadway before the Confidence bus got there, then you would have no other choice but to catch the second bus, which was King Alphonso. However, if you also missed the King Alphonso bus, then you would be out of luck because "home sweet home" would be your silent whisper. As for me, I was more than ready for the first bus that was scheduled to arrive that morning. Within a couple of minutes, the Confidence bus arrived and I signaled to the driver by waving my hand super vigorously. I waved goodbye to Aunt Lucy and Sister Lin, boarded the bus, and off I went to the Albert Town Secondary School.

The bus made many stops along the way. Although I did not take an official count of the number of passengers, I would say, for a vehicle that was designed to carry somewhere around fifty-five to sixty passengers, it had approximately eighty to ninety people on board at any given

The Alpha (α)

After thirty-four years, Albert Town High (formerly Albert Town Secondary) is still serving as a vital knowledge infusion to the community. As you can see, the motto speaks for itself.

time. The conductor was cramming people inside the bus like sardines in a can. There were passengers on the rooftop and several schoolchildren hanging off the steps. After many stops and several close calls with other motor vehicles, the bus finally arrived at Albert Town. As soon as the bus

The RICH acronym stands for Resourceful, Industrious, Courteous, and Honest

came to a stop, most of the passengers, including students and faculty members, started pushing and shoving to get off the bus.

Before I forget, let me share a little humor with you regarding a nightmare experience we, the passengers, had with one of the bus drivers. Our confidence was shaken when a maniac driver was assigned to our route. Everyone throughout the many communities the bus served addressed the driver as Speedy. I can assure you that this driver has taken his passengers to the precipice of hell many times. He

Chapter 3

sped around the corners as if he owned the road and there were absolutely no other vehicles coming from the opposite direction. Instead of stopping at a safe area to give way to oncoming traffic, he drove dangerously close to the edge of the precipice just to get by without stopping. I mean, the bus was so close to the edge that when I looked out the window, it appeared as though the bus was no longer on the road. For the entire journey, my heart would be pounding like a drum. Everyone was very happy when he was removed from our route. Even the older folks would sigh an enthusiastic, "Thank you, Jesus," when they boarded the bus and discovered that Speedy was no longer the driver.

Enough of Speedy; let me get back to my bright academic adventure. After getting off the bus, the students and faculty members walked briskly from the town square to the school, which was located approximately 200 yards from the town square. Seeing that this was my first day, I followed the crowd and navigated my way around until I found my classroom.

Just as I sat down and was about to relax, the bell rang. Once again, I just followed the crowd as everyone proceeded to a large open hall. As soon as the students were settled, Mr. Dodd, the school principal, commenced the morning's devotion by welcoming everyone to Albert Town Secondary School. He also outlined the agenda for the new school year and outlined our obligations as they related to the school policies.

After the introduction, he turned over the agenda to the school reverend, who conducted the religious portion of the morning's devotion. In Jamaica, devotion is a religious ritual that is deeply rooted in most schools' (private and public) curriculum. Unlike the United States,

The Alpha (α)

in Jamaica there is no real separation of church and state. Therefore, the church plays an integral role in the religious aspects of academic institutions. Most schools, including Albert Town Secondary, have a pastor or reverend on staff, acting in either a full-time or a part-time role.

After the morning's devotion, we dispersed to our assigned classes. Seeing that it was my first day, and being a total stranger to the routine, I chose to sit quietly in my seat and watch as the returning students chatted among themselves. After a good fifteen minutes of waiting, the instructor came into the classroom and commenced the day's session by welcoming us and outlining the agenda for the school year.

The academic process at the secondary schools was very much different from what I was accustomed to at the all-age schools. At the all-age academic level, the students are assigned to one classroom where they spent their entire school year being taught by one instructor, except for vocational sessions if available. However, at the secondary level, the students' school day is divided into sessions or clusters that are based on each subject. The sessions included math, English, science, religious education, social studies, and vocational studies. Most of the sessions are taught by different instructors and are located in different buildings across the campus.

Here is a quick overview of the school academic structure: While the seventh- through ninth-grade students spend most of their time on their academic coursework, the tenth- and eleventh-grade students spend anywhere from two to three days per week in their vocational areas. As it relates to the tenth- and eleventh-grade students, the extra vocational time was essential to allow for more

Chapter 3

real-world, hands-on training. It was mandatory for all the students at this level to attend classes in all subject areas, including their vocational training areas. As for me, I needed to enroll in a vocational skill that would allow me to work a regular job or become an independent contractor if necessary. Besides, I was looking forward to obtaining a skill that would prepare me for the work world right after graduation. After deep consideration and close consultation, I chose the Electrical Installation vocational career. And would you believe that this major turned out to be a "shocking" experience for me? Okay, not quite but . . .

The tenth-grade students were introduced to the different subject and vocational areas and the instructors who were assigned to each area. Mr. Morrison was my tenth-grade and eleventh-grade vocational instructor. He was also known as scooby/Scobie to the students. I am not sure about the spelling because no one had explained to me why he was tagged with that pet name. He was a calm, pleasant, and soft-spoken person. Not only that, but he only spoke when necessary; he was never distracted by the insignificant events, especially those triggered by the students.

Shortly after the introduction, the bell rang, and the students dispersed for lunch. After lunch, we resumed classes, which lasted for another two hours. Finally, school ended at 2:10 p.m. and most of the students and faculty members dispersed to their respective homes.

My going-home situation was a bit different. I had a choice between two buses, Confidence and King Alphonso. Both buses were scheduled to arrive anywhere between 4:30 and 6:00 p.m. Seeing that the distance between home and school was approximately eight miles,

The Alpha (α)

I had two choices, either to walk the eight miles home or to sit around and wait for one of the two buses to arrive. As I did not have a specific reason to get home before the arrival of the buses, I chose the latter. To make the best use of my time, I went to the public library to catch up on my reading. Not only that, but I needed to spend all of my free time on my schoolwork because I was suffering from a major academic deficit. To put it mildly, I was in the tenth grade, but my academic standing was more like that of the fifth-grade level.

I do not want to bore you with each day's activities, so instead I will summarize the major events. Monday through Wednesday, most of my time was consumed with the different subject areas, while Thursdays and Fridays were dedicated to my vocational training. As the weeks progressed, the schedule became routine, but the academic and the vocational training workload increased significantly. I spent a great deal of time studying the fundamentals of electricity, electrical circuitry, and related components. After we had grasped the theory and much of the practical, lab-related knowledge, we were allowed to work with Mr. Morrison on several electrical installation and maintenance projects.

School life became routine except for my vocational area, which had taken on many more practical training hours. On Thursdays and Fridays, instead of school, I would report to different job sites in Trelawny and Manchester. Although we were not being compensated financially, I can assure you that the knowledge we obtained far outweighed the financial cost. Therefore, I was by no means worried about the additional expense I incurred in this regard.

Chapter 3

Irrespective of where we were, we were expected to conduct ourselves in accordance with all of the academic policies and procedures. However, that did not stop us from pulling an occasional prank once in a while. Speaking about pranks, here is one that I would like to share with you. One day we noticed that Mr. Morrison had taken off his coverall and placed it within reach of students. With the phrase, "boys will be boys" fully enacted, one of the students placed several large rocks into Mr. Morrison's coverall pockets. Unaware of what had happened, Mr. Morrison put on the coverall and attempted to climb a ladder but was experiencing difficulty doing so. He quickly checked his coverall pockets and discovered that they were heavily laden with rocks. At first, he was not too happy with us for engaging in such silly behavior. However, the laughter was just too much for him not to join in the fun. Irrespective of the once-in-a-blue-moon childish acts, overall, we had lots of fun working on many hands-on projects with our favorite instructor, Mr. Morrison. I can assure you that this vocational training provided me with a wealth of knowledge that has contributed directly to my practical career even to this very day.

Financial Hiccup

Regardless of how economical my academic career appeared to have been, it became apparent that a financial problem was looming on the horizon. The weekly $15, plus the occasional meal allowance, could barely cover the basic school-related expenses, including transportation and food. To further compound the problem, I was now in need of textbooks and other supplies. Despite

The Alpha (α)

the financial constraints, Aunt Lucy was doing her best to make ends meet. I was excited about school regardless of the severe financial constraints. Just being able to attend school was a grand opportunity for me. However, it came at a cost and had significantly depleted Aunt Lucy's limited funds.

Approximately halfway through the first school year, my financial woes became even more apparent. I had to forego a number of the textbooks that were essential for me to complete the two-year program successfully. Not only that, but what happened next really added more doubt to my already bleak financial outlook. One Monday morning, when it came time for Aunt Lucy to provide me with my weekly allowance, I noticed that she went into the shop but did not return as promptly as she usually did. I walked into the shop and noticed that Aunt Lucy was shuffling around picking up all the available loose change to come up with the $15 for my weekly allowance. What really got my attention was when she said, "Desmond, here is the last $15 that I have in the shop, but I want you to take it and go to school." I accepted it reluctantly because I realized that I had become a financial liability to my foster mother.

She was now seventy years old and should have been enjoying her retirement years instead of having to worry about my everyday needs. Other than the small, intermittent financial help that she was receiving from the CDA and the occasional small remittance from family members living in the USA and the UK, Aunt Lucy had no real source of income. She had no pension fund, social security benefits, 401K, or any other form of retirement investment to live off. Moreover, she had long given up on the full-time

Chapter 3

operation of the grocery shop. In fact, she had scaled back the grocery shop operation to a very limited assortment of snacks, candies, and beverages. In other words, she was operating a tuck shop rather than a grocery store. With that said, I needed to strategize and come up with a viable economic alternative, because dropping out of school was not my first, second, or third option; neither was it Aunt Lucy's. Seeing that I was unable to do anything about my financial problem (at least for that moment), I took the money, thanked her, and went to school.

That day, my mind was preoccupied trying to come up with ways to reduce my spending. I had already enacted all of the cost-saving measures I could possibly think of, which meant that I was out of options. However, a little idea popped into my head, and it convinced me that if I had a bicycle, then I could ride it to and from school, thus eliminating the need to ride the bus. I must admit that I also thought it would be an exciting adventure to ride a bicycle to and from school. With that said, I started saving my lunch money toward a bicycle.

After approximately two weeks of not eating lunch, I quickly realized that this cost-cutting method was unrealistic; I would have to forgo too many lunches just to save enough to buy a bicycle. Moreover, I was too darn hungry to concentrate on my schoolwork in the afternoons. With that said, I was now in need of some income, because cost-cutting alone was definitely not going to solve my financial debacle. To paraphrase Washington lawmakers, I needed to implement a "fiscally balanced approach."

One afternoon while I was in class, a little thought popped into my head, and it said, "Why not use land at home to cultivate vegetables and sell them to the people of the community?" The more I thought about this idea, the more feasible it became. There were three main reasons why this idea was a realistic approach. First, none of the farmers from the community were cultivating vegetables. Second, the people of the community were traveling eight, thirteen, and sometimes many more miles just to purchase their produce. Third, if adopted, this venture would provide me with the additional funds I needed while proving a lot more economical for the residents of the community. In my mind, this plan was the pot of gold at the end of the rainbow. With all the indicators trending upward, I was convinced that cultivating vegetables and selling them to the locals was precisely the solution to my financial problem.

Now that I had conceived this visionary plan, the real question was how I would go about getting financial assistance to cover the startup costs associated with this venture. I realized that I needed to strategize some more. However, the first week went by, and I did not have a clue how I was going to get over this financial hurdle.

The Financial Breakthrough

What I am about to explain is one more reminder that there is always a silver lining among the darkest clouds. This silver lining was revealed while I was attending one of my classes. As I sat there, I found myself juggling many thoughts in my mind. Suddenly a little voice popped into my head and said, "Why don't you ask Aunt Carmen to send you some vegetable seeds?" Aunt Carmen, who was one of Aunt Lucy's nieces residing in England, was the first person who came to my mind because of a dramatic scene I created at the airport the night she and her daughter

Chapter 3

visited Jamaica. I will definitely fill you in on the detail of this airport drama later. Anyway, I took a pen and a sheet of paper and wrote a letter to Aunt Carmen. I do not recall the exact words or phrases I used, however, I asked her if she could please send me some vegetable seeds so that I could establish a vegetable business and use the proceeds to cover my school expenses. At the time, I had no idea if it was feasible for her to ship vegetable seeds from England to Jamaica, but nonetheless, I decided to press ahead with my plan.

As soon as I got home, I went straight into the shop and greeted Aunt Lucy with a pleasant, "Good evening, Aunt Lucy." I wanted to come right out and asked her for Aunt Carmen's address, but I was a bit hesitant. Despite my reservations, I went ahead and expressed my concerns to her regarding our financial problems, and how I would address them by cultivating and selling vegetables to the locals. I also explained to her that I would use the proceeds to purchase a bicycle that I could ride to school instead of relying on public transportation. Aunt Lucy told me that she did not approve of my riding some sixteen miles each day to and from school due to the risks involved. However, despite her reservations in that regard, she gave her approval for the vegetable aspect of my proposal. With that said, I told her that I was thinking of asking Aunt Carmen to ship some vegetable seeds from England. Aunt Lucy agreed and provided me with Aunt Carmen's address. As soon as she gave me the mailing address, I jotted it down on the envelope and mailed it. Now that my part was completed, all I had to do was to sit and wait for Aunt Carmen to respond.

The Alpha (α)

The land that I once used to cultivate my vegetables.
See more photos at the www.fosteringthroughtheeyesofachild.net website.

After waiting patiently for a couple of weeks, lo and behold, one day I received a package in the mail. Sure enough, it was the package that I had been eagerly awaiting. Aunt Carmen had sent me several containers of vegetable seeds and onion bulbs. I can assure you that this was a very blessed day for me! Although I had not received any formal training in the art of growing vegetables, I set out to use the little knowledge I had gained while observing my father as he cultivated his vegetable gardens and, yes, even his favorite marijuana plantations. Also, I incorporated the hands-on knowledge I had acquired from cultivating my little vegetable gardens while living with my former foster parents. I combined a little know-how, common-sense approach along the way as well. I did not have to worry about where I would

Chapter 3

cultivate vegetables because Aunt Lucy had more than enough land.

Having acquired the vegetable seeds and the land, it was now a matter of how I would organize the limited time I had so that I could cultivate enough vegetables to sustain a business. The limited amount of time I had was attributable to the inconvenient bus schedule, which arrived about 7:00 a.m. and returned at 5:00 p.m. This schedule was contingent upon the day of the week and the weather conditions. That is, there was a strong probability that I could leave for school around 7:00 a.m. and never return home until 7:00 p.m. Therefore, this schedule did not leave me with enough daylight hours to plant the desired amount of vegetable to sustain a business. The weekend (Saturday) was just not enough time to do all my other chores and take care of the vegetable garden. Moreover, I could not do any gardening on Sunday because it was considered a day of rest.

Despite the time constraints, I decided to get going with my vegetable venture. I started that weekend by dividing the land into small plots to accommodate the different types of vegetables. I set aside plots for cabbage, callaloo, carrots, bell peppers (sweet pepper, as per Jamaicans), radishes, cucumbers, green beans (string beans), tomatoes, onions, and bok choy (or pop chow, as per Jamaicans). When I had divvied up the land, it was time for me to prepare the beds for sowing the seeds. However, I soon realized that not having water to support irrigation had become my biggest problem. There was no running water in the village; therefore, everyone had to rely on Mother Nature to water their farms and for their everyday water needs.

The Alpha (α)

Most of the residents used tanks, drums, barrels, or containers that could be filled with rainwater that ran off their roofs. There was also a very large public water tank but I could not use that water for farming because the residents who did not have any water tank relied on the public water facility for their everyday needs. Now it dawned on me that insufficient water was the main reason why no one in the community cultivated enough vegetables to sustain a business. Without irrigation, my vegetable endeavor seemed rather impossible.

Instead of giving up hope, I decided to turn to a higher being for help. With that said, I prayed and asked the Lord to bless my garden and to make it fruitful, or vegeful depending on your scientific rationale. I remember opening up my little New Testament Bible, and Psalm 128:2 was the scripture that jumped right out at me. It reads, "For thou shalt eat the labor of thine hands: happy shalt thou be, and it shall be well with thee" (KJV). After reading this Bible verse, I never again found myself worrying about not having an irrigation system. In retrospect, after seeing the overwhelming results that were attributed to Psalm 128:2, I wonder what would have happened if I had read Psalm 128:3.

After I was through praying and reading my favorite scripture, I sowed the seeds. Then I took a little of the water from Aunt Lucy's tank and used it to wet the soil lightly. I also harvested banana and plantain leaves and used them to cover the areas where the seeds had been sown. What was the rationale for covering the soil with banana and plantain leaves? I did not find this information in a book but, instead, learned this technique from

Chapter 3

observing my father while he was preparing his vegetable and marijuana seedbeds.

After sowing the first set of seeds in good soil (Biblical reference intended), I waited patiently for them to grow. After approximately three to four days, I peeked under the leaves and, *voilà*, the seeds had started germinating. After another day or two, I removed the leaves and continued to wet the soil lightly so that the daytime heat would not scorch the plants before they had a chance to take root fully. I had to use the water very sparingly because of the little water we had was a very precious commodity. This was even more critical throughout the dry months. There were times when I was unable to use any of the water from the tank because there was just not enough to support daily consumption and irrigation. I would like to emphasize that throughout such times, I found myself praying for dark clouds. Sorry, Jimmy Cliff, but your lyrics, "I can see clearly now the rain is gone," was certainly not my fantasy.

Despite the limited water, my foster mother, I, and the residents of the district were all amazed to see how the plants withstood the heat and remained green and healthy, as if they were receiving a daily dose of water. I did not go searching for a scientific explanation because I knew that God had done the watering and the nurturing for me. Based on my experience, I believe wholeheartedly that if you desire to achieve something good, and you have committed your passion to the Lord through prayer, then the Lord will reward your hard work. In life, there are certain experiences that science will not be able to explain, which is why everyone has to have a measure of faith that reminds us that there is a God. Besides, if you ever

The Alpha (α)

find yourself wondering if there is a God, then if possible, please try to recall an event or something that took place at a given point in your life that would remind you that there has to be a more superior being than humankind. Please see Appendix A for details concerning another event that took place while I was living at the orphanage.

So here are the details of how I was able to take care of my vegetable gardens without sacrificing any of my school time. First, I knew that leaving home at 7:00 a.m. in the mornings and returning home anywhere between 5:00 p.m. and 7:00 p.m. in the evenings did not leave me with enough time for gardening. Therefore, instead of waiting around for the bus after school, I decided to walk, jog, and run approximately eight miles home. It would take me approximately one and a half hours to get home in the evenings, thus giving me an additional two to three hours of daylight to work.

On rare occasions, or on my lucky days, I would steal a ride on one of the trucks that transported food products or other materials on that route. In fact, I used to steal rides from just about any motor vehicle that I could latch myself onto. I know you might be asking, how could it be possible for me to get onto a moving vehicle? Picture this: There I was walking, sometimes running or jogging, home from school with my ears tuned to my surroundings. Out of nowhere, I would hear a truck horn and engine bellowing through the Cockpit Mountains. After processing all that information, I concluded that a heavily-laden truck was approaching, going in my direction. I would then run to one of the rugged, semi-circle corners (which were not too hard to find) and wait there for the truck to arrive. Remember, we are not talking about a highway;

Chapter 3

we are talking about a winding country road where the end of one corner is the beginning of the next. As soon as the truck arrived at the corner and slowed to a crawl, I leaped onto it like a creature with suction-cup tentacles. After enduring the hellish ride for approximately four to six miles, I would hop off at a similar corner close to my home. I am quite sure that Aunt Lucy would have had a stern reprimand for me if she had found out that I was indulging in such risky behavior.

There were times when the additional daylight hours were just not enough for me to do all my gardening. However, I would make up the time by working early in the morning and late into the night with the aid of the moonlight. I remember Aunt Lucy would come by and say, "Desmond, it is time to put away the tools and come inside now, man." I would reply, "Soon come, Aunt Lucy," then I would go right back to my gardening the minute Aunt Lucy went back into the house. Even the neighbors would come by to see if I was really tending my vegetable garden at that time of the night. After a short conversation, they would have a good laugh and say, "Bwoy, farmer nuh wok a night!" ("Boy, farmers do not work at night!") I would respond by letting them know that I had been assigned to the night shift.

Sometimes I would recite my favorite Henry Wadsworth Longfellow proverb, "Heights by great men reached and kept were not attained by sudden flight, but they while their companions slept, were toiling upward in the night." Even to this very day, this is still one of my favorite phrases. I find it far more uplifting than the more depressing "Jack and Jill," "Humpty Dumpty," and "Ring around the Rosy" nursery rhymes I was taught in kindergarten. However, I would like to tweak one word from Mr. Longfellow's famous nursery rhyme to say "great people" instead of "great men."

Working in the early mornings and, yes, even at nights with the aid of the moonlight was among the rigorous measures I enacted to accomplish my objective. Within six to eight weeks, a number of the vegetables were ready for harvest. It was time to start marketing my produce to the people of the district. First, I initiated a word-of-mouth marketing campaign by announcing to the neighbors that, the following week, I would have fresh vegetables for sale. Aunt Lucy and Sister Lin joined in my marketing campaign and passed the word along as well. Most of the people in the district were fully aware, because my vegetable gardens were visible from the main road. Moreover, they had seen and heard me working in the field day in and day out, sometimes night in and night out as well.

The First Harvest

The weekend finally arrived, and the first order of business was for me to construct a makeshift grocery stand where customers would be able to purchase their vegetables. After I had everything in place, two of my neighbors, Christine and Sadie, came by and made a substantial purchase. That day, Aunt Lucy was quite busy announcing my vegetable business to her customers and the passersby. I became the beneficiary of her robust marketing campaign because shortly after that, people from the neighborhood started coming by to purchase vegetables. We sold more than $15 worth of vegetables that weekend. In fact, Aunt

Chapter 3

Lucy stopped keeping a tab on the revenue after we had exceeded the $15 margin. I was overwhelmed to know that I had exceeded my own expectations, and this sale constituted only a fraction of my vegetables. With this ROI, if my company had been publicly traded, the stock price would have gone through the roof. Where was Wall Street when I needed an IPO? No need to "speculate," just smile, nod, and move on.

By the second week, when the news had permeated the district, my customer base more than doubled. By the end of the fourth week, we had a little over $87 cash on hand, and that was after deducting my $15 weekly allowance. The word-of-mouth advertisement campaign continued to spread, and people started coming from other neighboring districts (Mahogany Hall and Alps) to buy vegetables from my garden. The vegetable business grew to the point that the more I reaped the vegetables such as tomatoes, callaloos, peppers, and cucumbers, the more they continued to bring forth even greater yield.

However, due to the demand, I found myself spending more time than planned tending the gardens. Aunt Lucy became a bit concerned and reminded me that I should not sacrifice any more of my time taking on extra gardening activities because attending school was my highest priority. Her philosophy was that the vegetable business is a means to provide me with the necessary financial resources to stay in school, not a money-making venture to keep me out of school. In other words, she was letting me know that as long as my academic expenses were met, it is not necessary to keep up with the demand. Today, I am very grateful for her words of wisdom because she never let me deviate or lose sight of my long-term goals, especially those about my academic career.

With this financial blessing, I took ownership of all my expenses, not only those related to my academic career. Now that I was able to afford all the necessary textbooks, I would spend a tremendous amount of time studying so that I could get caught up with my subjects. Most nights I would be up until 2:00 a.m. and sometimes 4:00 a.m. studying. On a number of occasions, Aunt Lucy would say to me, "Desmond, why are you up this hour of the night for, man?" My answer to her was always the same: "Studying, Aunt Lucy." I did not explain to her why it was important for me to stay up all night studying. However, after a while, she realized that for me to succeed academically, I needed to do just that.

I know I have said this earlier, but I believe that it is worth repeating. Everyone, including me, was amazed by the yield from the vegetable gardens. And with such a revelation, how could I ever be persuaded that there is not a God! I am quite sure that I would have given up if science was all I had. However, my deep abiding faith in God, the will to persevere, and Aunt Lucy's encouragement were the attributes that kept me going. This is another categorical assurance why I believe that faith and science are inseparable and indispensable. In other words, faith is not governed by science; instead, faith provides the will to persevere even in situations where the scientific odds seem impossible. With that said, I firmly believe that we should not discredit science, neither should we use scientific evidence to discredit or disprove the existence of God.

Chapter 3

Another lesson I learned from this outcome is one that reminds me that there are times when a person, or even our parents, might not be able to fulfill all of our needs. However, I do hope that we, especially the younger generation, should graciously accept the sacrifices that were made on our behalf. For example, if you need five things and you have been given two, then do not turn to those who gave you the two and let them know that you are still in need of three more. Always try your very best to build upon the foundation that others have laid for you. Finally, please remember that a seed cannot grow and flourish if you do not do your part, first sowing it and then spending a little time nurturing it. In other words, blessings do not come out of thin air or exist in a vacuum.

CHAPTER 4

REUNITED WITH MY BIOLOGICAL FAMILY

One day, while Aunt Lucy and I were at home conversing (hard to believe when compared with my former foster parents), all of a sudden she changed the conversation and said, "Desmond, I would like you to meet your parents so that you can talk to dem." At first, I did not take her suggestion seriously because none of us had any definitive information regarding my biological family's whereabouts. Moreover, I had not seen them in almost nine years, so the possibilities of their whereabouts could be endless. In fact, the only clue I had was based on my brother's recent visit and the assumption that, if they were alive and still in Jamaica, most likely they would be residing in the parish of Westmoreland.

Nevertheless, I told Aunt Lucy that I would be very happy if I could meet my parents someday. Although I was not too optimistic that I would ever see them again, deep down in my heart, I knew that meeting them would constitute a special moment for me. Besides, this would provide me with the opportunity to converse with them in an adult-like manner and to be able to ask them about

Chapter 4

many things. The conversation lasted only for a couple of minutes because I did not have much to contribute.

Approximately three months later, while Aunt Lucy and I were sitting in the grocery shop engaging in one of our usual conversations, she said, "Desmond, I am going to contact Leighton, and ask him to come down next week so that we can try and find your family." I remember asking myself, "Is Aunt Lucy seriously going to follow through with her promise? Why would she cause Leighton, her grandnephew, to drive all the way from Kingston to Sawyers to take me on a wild goose chase in search of a family whom I had not seen or heard from in almost nine years?" I did not want Aunt Lucy to take on such an enormous responsibility, so I tried not to look or sound too enthusiastic. Moreover, I had no idea if this undertaking would be approved by the CDA. Although it would be a delight for me to be reunited with my parents, I did not want anything, not even my biological parents, to interfere with or disrupt the wonderful relationship I had with my foster mother.

Even though I was not displaying any enthusiasm with regard to Aunt Lucy's proposal, she continued the conversation by asking, "Desmond, do you know where you were born?" Although I was not entirely sure, I told her that I had been born in Westmoreland because I remember living there with my father throughout my early childhood years. I also told her that, at one point, I had lived with my mother in a district know as Logwood, which is located in the parish of Hanover. She took a little book and recorded the information, and that was where our conversation ended for that day.

Later that week, Aunt Lucy contacted Leighton, and he agreed to come by the following weekend. I am not sure if Aunt Lucy had explained to Leighton the nature of this trip, because none of us had any idea how a journey such as this would unfold. Regardless of the challenges that lay ahead, the following weekend, as promised, Leighton drove from Kingston to Sawyers to take us on this "Alice in Wonderland" journey. Sunday morning, bright and early, Leighton, Aunt Lucy, and I headed out for Westmoreland in search of my parents. Leighton was the perfect candidate for this undertaking because he was a member of the Jamaican police force and happened to be familiar with most, if not all, of the parishes, including Westmoreland and Hanover. As for me, I was not too optimistic that this endeavor would bring about a happy ending. However, Aunt Lucy was confident that if my parents were alive, then Leighton would be able to find them. If Leighton were unable to locate my parents, then I could pretty much give up on finding them. In fact, I would go as far as to say, if you turn over a rock in any of the parishes, Leighton would tell you exactly what is under that rock. Okay, I am stretching it, but you get the point.

The Search Engines That Never Quit

After driving for approximately two hours, we made our first stop in Logwood, Hanover. We drove all over Logwood asking anyone and everyone we came across if they knew Ivene or Iah. Ivene and Iah are my mother and father's Rastafarian names, which were all I had to go by. After making many stops and many inquiries, it seemed as though no

Chapter 4

one had the slightest clue regarding the two individuals we were inquiring about. This limited knowledge made it very difficult for anyone to assist us. Nevertheless, Aunt Lucy and Leighton (more so Aunt Lucy) were not about to give up, and with much determination and perseverance, they continued their search. We searched for over four hours but came up empty-handed. I wish I had other search terms because Ivene and Iah kept returning, "No family member found." Where were Facebook, Twitter, Snapchat, and Instagram when we needed a few social networks?

After driving around for another hour, Leighton decided to expand our search beyond Logwood. With that said, he drove from Hanover to Westmoreland. Just as we were going through Haddow (a little district in the parish of Westmoreland), we came across a group of young men who were sitting on a stone wall along the roadway, relaxing for the afternoon. Leighton stopped the car, stepped out, went over to where they were sitting, and started conversing with them. After a brief discussion, Leighton signaled to me to get out of the car and join him so that the group of young men could speak with me directly. The minute I approached them, I overheard one of them say, "Yeah man, a Little Gal youth dat man. An yuh nuh deh far yuh nuh, Little Gal lib up pan da hill deh," while pointing up the hill. In plain English, what he actually said was, "Yes man, you are indeed Little Gal's son. Also, you are not too far away because she lives on top of that hill." I thanked them, and with no further delay, I commenced my journey up the winding, rocky trail.

Seeing that I had not received the exact address, I decided that it would be a good idea to stop and ask for directions. (And just in case you did not know, guys do ask for direction too.) With that said, I stopped and asked a woman who was standing at the entrance of her house (let's go with the assumption that it was her house) for directions. "Mam," I asked, "do you know where Ivene lives?" The woman paused for a moment as if she were not familiar with the name Ivene. Although I really did not want to address my mother as "Little Gal," I did so just to see if she knew who I was inquiring about. Immediately after that, she pointed in the direction of a little board structure approximately 250 feet away. The expression on the woman's face led me to believe that she had a vague idea who I was but refrained from asking. I thanked her and continued along the path she had indicated.

Miraculous Reunification

Upon arrival, I saw a very skinny woman standing by the doorway of a little outdoor kitchen. Looking at her, it made perfect sense why everyone addressed her as Little Gal. She was, indeed a very tiny person. I approached her and said, "Good afternoon, mam," and she replied likewise. "Are you Ivene?" I asked, and with no hesitation, she replied, "Yes." Then I said to her, "Come with me, there is someone down the road who would like to speak with you." Although I did not provide her with the reason, she did accordingly.

Although I recognized my mother's distinctive voice, I was unable to conclude definitively that the person to whom I was speaking was indeed my mother. The most depressing outcome was that my mother did not recognize that I was her son. There we were, like two strangers walking down the rocky pathway that led to the main

Chapter 4

road. I did not give her any clue of who I was, neither did she ask. However, the suspense blew wide open when the same curious woman whom I had asked for directions said to my mother, "Little Gal, a mine da bwoy de fayva yuh son so?" ("Little Gal, that boy resembles your son.") Immediately, my mother turned, looked at me, and said, "Desmond! Oh, Desmond, mi son. Long time mi nu si yuh mi couldn't mek yuh out a tall." ("Desmond! Oh, Desmond, my son, I have not seen you in such a long time I did not recognize you.") I remember saying to her, "Yes, Ivene, I am your son." After the excitement was over, we continued down the path to the main road. Upon arrival, I introduced her to Aunt Lucy, then I stepped aside so that they could talk.

I did not want to listen in on their conversation, but I could not help myself because I was quite curious to hear what my mother had to say. I overheard my mother passing all the blame onto my father for everything that had happened to us, her children. She also stated that my father was the reason why Pauline, Paulette, George, and I had been taken from their care and placed in orphanages. She did not bear any of the responsibility at all. Based on my observations, I knew that Aunt Lucy was not trying to determine whose fault it was but was merely trying to uncover the facts as they related to the family structure and whereabouts. Therefore, Aunt Lucy changed the subject and started asking my mother more general questions regarding the family as a whole.

Throughout the rest of their conversation, my mother told Aunt Lucy that, in addition to Pauline and Paulette, I also had two other sisters, Inez and Gracie. She also told Aunt Lucy that Inez, Gracie, Pauline, and Paulette were currently living in Montego Bay. She did not mention my brother in any of her conversations. However, she told us that once we located Inez, she would be able to provide us with the necessary information regarding the rest of the family. Aunt Lucy promised my mother that she would allow me to come back and spend some time with her very soon. I was not overwhelmed with any great emotion because everything was like a blur, and I was busy trying to understand what had just transpired. After my mother and Aunt Lucy were through conversing, we waved goodbye and commenced our journey to Montego Bay to locate Inez. My mother asked Scubby, one of Inez's siblings (by her mother's side), to accompany us to Inez's home.

Meeting My Eldest Sibling for the First Time

We drove to Inez's home, which was located in the West Green housing complex in Montego Bay, St. James. Upon arrival, Scubby got out of the car, ran to the gate, and shouted, "Sis!" several times. Shortly after that, a woman came out of the house, and Scubby said to her, "Sis, si yuh bredda yah." ("Sister, here is your brother.") We both looked at each other, but neither of us seemed to have a clue who the other person really was. Not to prolong the inevitable, I went ahead and explained to her who I was and let her know that my mother (Ivene) told me that she was my sister. With no further hesitation, Inez said, "Desmond! Oh, my God! Mi try fi fine yuh an yuh bredda fi years but cudden fine unnu." ("Desmond! Oh, my God! I tried to find you and your brother for years but could not.") She then invited us inside and offered us something to drink. I was overwhelmed with joy to be meeting my sister, whom

Chapter 4

I had not seen or heard of before. It was not easy for me to comprehend that much revelation in such a short time.

Inez told me that she was thirty-two years old and that she had a son, Lorenzo (Mackey), and a daughter, Cassandra (Donnette). I did not get to meet them because they had gone to church. She also told me that Pauline and Paulette were living in Tucker, a little district located in the parish of St. James. Then she told me that I had another sister, Grace, on my father's side, who was thirty-one and currently living with her two children, Michael and Sherene, in Mount Salem, Montego Bay. Finally, she told me that my mother's name was Vivian Robinson and hers was Euphema Tomlinson. That was refreshing to know because, up to that point, I had thought that my mother's real name was Ivene. Once again, I noticed that she did not mention George. My only rationale was that nobody wanted to provide me with the depressing news regarding my brother. They may have thought that it was not appropriate to overshadow my joy by letting me know that my brother had returned to the Rastafarian lifestyle and was suffering from mental illness.

Just as I was getting acquainted with my sister, it was time for us to leave because Leighton had a long drive back to Kingston. The long drive was attributable to the poor condition of the road, which was littered with potholes and an endless number of curves.[7] Before leaving for home, Aunt Lucy promised Inez that she would allow me to spend some time with her and the rest of the family

---

7 Today the road is much better due to significant improvements that have been undertaken by the Jamaican and Chinese governments. A journey that once took approximately three hours can now be accomplished in under an hour. And the good thing is that your vehicle remains intact after the journey.

during the summer holidays. With that said, we waved goodbye and commenced our trip home.

Throughout the rest of the journey, my mind was fully preoccupied with the sequence of events that had unfolded in such a short period. It was beyond my wildest imagination that I would someday have the opportunity to be reunited with my mother, much less to be united with two of my older sisters, whom I had never seen or heard about before. For many years, I had no clue if I would ever be reunited with my family, but all that had changed in a single day. I owed it to the relentless perseverance and determination of Aunt Lucy and Leighton. Step aside, Google, Bing, Facebook, Instagram, Snapchat; these two individuals are my most trusted search engines and social networks.

After a long, tiresome, but rewarding day's journey, we finally made it back to Sawyers. Now that I was home, I needed a healthy meal and lots of rest to recoup. However, that was only wishful thinking because I was so overwhelmed by the day's events, I simply could not eat nor could I sleep. And from that point forward, my life was never the same.

Off to Visit My Mother and Siblings

Finally, the long-awaited summer of 1985 arrived, and Aunt Lucy lived up to her promise by arranging for me to go and spend two weeks with my mother and sisters. I packed a little bag with the necessities and waited eagerly for daybreak. I got up very early that Saturday morning, dressed, hurried to the kitchen, and greeted Aunt Lucy with a pleasant "Good morning, Aunt Lucy." She replied

Chapter 4

likewise and offered me a delicious breakfast, which I ate quickly. After breakfast, I went by the roadway and waited impatiently for the bus to arrive. I was very excited knowing that this opportunity would allow me to spend quality time with my family, especially my mother. Within a couple of minutes, I heard the bus horn echoing through the Cockpit Mountains. I signaled to the driver by waving my hand vigorously. He stopped the bus and I bid one last goodbye to Aunt Lucy and Sister Lin, boarded the bus, and was off to Montego Bay. I was not sure exactly where I was going, but I knew that once the bus arrived in Montego Bay, then I would be able to find Inez's home. Although I did not have the actual address, I still had a good idea based on my first visit.

The bus drove through several neighborhoods, picking up and letting off passengers. After a long and bumpy ride, we finally arrived in Montego Bay. I got off at the final stop, which is the open farmer's market. After asking several individuals for directions, I finally found my sister's house. She was not at home, but I met my niece and nephew, Donnette and Mackey. I introduced myself, and they were very happy to see me. With no hesitation, my nephew took me to his mom's workplace. She was busy tending to her customers, but the minute she saw us, she hurried over and greeted me with a big and pleasant smile. She then turned to the customers who were in the bar and in a rather high-pitched voice said, "Unnu watch yah, a mi bredda dis yuh nuh!" ("Guys and gals, this is my brother!") I could see the joy radiating from her face. She then shouted in a jovial manner at a man who operated a little jerk stand (grill) and said, "Jerky, fix up two lunch fi mi deh!" ("Jerky, please prepare two lunches for me!")

Mr. Jerky prepared the lunches and gave them to Mackey and me. Over the years, I learned that making sure that we never went hungry was always a top priority for my sister. As a matter of fact, whenever you happened to be around her, one of her very first questions would be, "Yuh hungry?" And just before you provided her with a yes or no answer, she would have already ordered a meal and had it waiting for you.

Later that afternoon, I met my twin sisters, Pauline and Paulette (I-line and I-lette). It was a wonderful experience to be reunited with my sisters, whom I had not seen or heard from in almost nine years. That day I also met Gracie, one of my elder sisters, whom I had never met before. I also had the opportunity of meeting her son and her daughter, Michael and Sherene. I was seventeen when I met Inez and Gracie for the very first time. As for Pauline and Paulette, we had been separated when the police officers raided my father's home, took us away, and placed us in different orphanages.

The Much-anticipated Reunion

After spending the first week among my sisters, I boarded a minivan and was finally on my way to spend the most anticipated time of my life with my mother. Even to this very day, I am struggling to find the right words to express my emotions and how much I was really looking forward to a day like this. Having the opportunity to be reunited with my mother was a dream come true. As for the journey, there was no need for me to be concerned because I had a visual map of her home etched in my memory. After a rollercoaster-like journey, the minivan finally made it to Line

Chapter 4

Gate/Haddow. Just as the minivan was about to go around the steep corner that I used as my landmark, I signaled to the driver, "One stap, driva." As soon as the minivan came to a stop, I got off and walked briskly up the steep slope to my mother's home.

Upon arrival, I saw my mother coming out of the little kitchen that was adjacent to the house. In retrospect, one would wonder why my mother was so skinny considering the amount of time she spent in her kitchen. As I approached the house, my mother turned and looked at me, but I could clearly see that she did not recognize me right away. Or it could have been that she was a bit surprised because she had no clue that I was coming to visit her. However, she recognized me the minute I greeted her with a hearty "Good morning, Ivene." I did not greet my mother in the usual mother-son (mummy, mom, etc.) manner because of the traumatic experience I had while living with my former foster parents.

My mother greeted me, which was a vast difference to what had transpired on my first visit. We greeted each other more like two friends. Although I had no knowledge of what a motherly bond is like, I am quite sure that the experiences I had with my mother that day did not display any of the mother-and-child characteristics that I have witnessed between other children and their parents. Nevertheless, after the short meet and greet, my mother told me to go and have a seat on a little wooden bench on the verandah. I did accordingly but was hoping that she would come and join me as soon as possible so that we could get going with our long-overdue conversation.

After a couple of minutes, my mother presented me with breakfast. I had already eaten but rejecting my mother's breakfast was surely not the way to commence our reunion. With that in mind, I accepted it and ate it graciously. From what I can remember, breakfast consisted of a fried dumpling (more like a leftover dumpling from the previous day's meal that had been fried) and a cup of coffee. Wait! No meat? You mean the breakfast had zero protein? Yep, that's it! Well, I hope my mother had used protein-enriched flour. If this was her everyday diet, then it's no wonder why she was so skinny.

After breakfast, I was eager to discuss essential family matters with my mother. I started with a few basic parent-to-child inquires. However, my mother was unable to answer any of my questions. For instance, I asked her what year I was born and, to my surprise, she told me that she did not have a clue. She also did not have a clue how old my siblings were either. The same went for all the other questions that a mother should have had some knowledge of concerning her children. That was when it dawned on me that my mother had to be suffering from severe amnesia or was not interested in talking about her children or anything regarding the past. She also gave me the impression that she was not interested in talking about my brother, either.

I found out later that George had a stern conversation with our mother about deserting us, especially throughout our childhood years. This desertion was undoubtedly the main reason why the motherly bond was just not there. Although it was a very painful experience for me, from that point forward, I resorted to only having general conversations with my mother. That is, our conversation was similar to that of two friends indulging in casual chitchat. I spent four days with my mother and then went back to

Chapter 4

Montego Bay, where I spent another night with my sisters. The following day, I boarded the King Alphonso bus and went back home.

Upon arrival, Aunt Lucy was very excited to see me and was quite eager to hear about my trip, primarily the time I had spent with my mother. However, the feedback I provided her concerning the time I had spent with my mother was not what she was anticipating. Nonetheless, Aunt Lucy was still happy to know that I was able to spend some time with my siblings more so my mother.

After many visits with my mother, I concluded that my mother seemed not to display any mother-child relationship. For example, she would answer my questions very briefly with no enthusiasm or concern that I addressed her as Ivene and not as mom or mummy. That was when it dawned on me that the motherly bond I was searching for was just not there, and I needed to come to terms with reality and move on. Knowing that I was unable to establish a bond with my mother is one of the lost opportunities that keep me up at night. Although I had not discussed this outcome with George, based on what he told me, I am quite sure he felt the same way.

I am not casting the blame solely on my mother, because I came to realize that a parent-child emotional bond is not one that can be turned on and off like a light switch, nor can it be regulated like a valve. If it is not there, then it is simply not there. Regardless of the missing motherly bond, overall, I was delighted that Aunt Lucy had provided me with the opportunity to be reunited with my mother and my siblings. Besides, I was happy to have met my nieces and nephews for the very first time.

It took another twenty-five years before I was able to understand a little more concerning my mother's personality. My cousin Vyroline and I were having a jovial conversation when she turned to me and said, "You are a jovial person just like your mother." Something told me that she knew more about my mother than I had initially thought. I was quite eager to hear more. Unfortunately, our conversation ended prematurely due to time constraints. Next time we spoke, I asked her to fill me in on the type of person my mother had been. And that was when she told me that my mother was a loving, kind, compassionate, and jovial person. She also said that whenever she was feeling down, my mother was always there to comfort her. I understand that it is difficult to summarize a person's life traits in just one short conversation, however, that one conversation I had with my cousin brought me one step closer to knowing the type of person my mother had been. That is, a bond that I had not been able to experience throughout the time I spent with my mother, because our lives were always about survival on the run.

Even at the orphanage, I spent many days yearning that someday my brother and I would be reunited with our family but instead, we were transferred to a foster home. Unfortunately, the foster parents who had been entrusted to love and care for us denied us our childhood dreams. Although nothing can replace the love that I never experienced as a child, today the fatherly love I share with my daughters and the motherly love I witness between them and their mother has brought me one step closer to my lost childhood.

CHAPTER 5

WHAT'S NEXT

Crossing the Finish Line

Now that I was back home after such a life-changing experience, it was time to buckle down and complete the rest of my academic studies at Albert Town Secondary (now Albert Town High). After spending another year in school, I finally made it to the end of my academic and vocational studies. The day of my graduation arrived, and Aunt Lucy and most of the church brothers and sisters were in attendance. I was recognized for being the most improved and most cooperative student. I am not sure why I was awarded for being the most cooperative student, but as for the most improved, that accomplishment I earned through many, many hours of all-night studying and the blessings of the Lord that transformed my vegetable business into a successful venture. Also, none of this would be possible without Aunt Lucy and the people of Sawyers and the surrounding districts who had been my loyal customers. This recognition was a clear indication that my hard work and relentless perseverance had not gone unnoticed. Once again, this certainly would have been my brother's

Chapter 5

accomplishment if he had been given the opportunity to live out his life's dream.

Life after Albert Town Secondary School

Although I had reached the end of my academic journey from an economic perspective, I could hear a persistent voice telling me that this was only just the beginning. Despite the upbeat voice that was buzzing around inside my head, I had to come to terms with reality and learn to take life one day at a time. Moreover, I did not know what lies ahead, nor did I have the slightest clue what the next phase of my life's journey would be. I must also admit that I found myself, at times, wishing that I had the necessary resources to further my academic career. However, I have learned over the years that I should not worry about the things I have no control over because worrying has never solved any of my problems, nor has it ever provided me with any meaningful solutions. Even with that assurance, I still find myself worrying a lot more than I should.

With not much that I could do from a financial perspective, I decided to once again put my hope and trust in God. Despite the overwhelming financial odds, there was yet another golden academic and career opportunity, which turned out to be the Human Employment and Resource Training Trust.[8] To paint a complete picture of

---

[8] The Human Employment and Resource Training (HEART) Trust was established in 1982. HEART is financed through a compulsory 3-percent payroll deduction levied on qualified private sector firms, which is supplemented by assistance from international partners. The trust is mandated to finance, develop, and monitor employment-training programs, assist in placing graduates seeking jobs, and promote employment projects. Training is

What's Next

this life-changing, destined-to-be opportunity, I will have to revisit a point in time while I was a student at Albert Town Secondary School.

There I was, minding my own business, walking along the corridor that led to the vocational building. My whole "minding my own business" was interrupted when I turned my head in the direction of the administration offices and my line-of-sight collided with that of Mr. Levy, who was one of the instructors. Knowing that it was not good manners (as taught by my former foster mother) to make direct eye contact with an adult, I quickly turned my head in the direction I was going and continued walking along the corridor. Just before I exited the corridor, I heard someone behind me yelling, "Young man, young man!" The minute I turned my head, I saw Mr. Levy coming toward me. I paused for a moment and looked directly at him as he approached me. As soon as he was within talking distance, he said to me in a rather stern voice, "Young man! I said, come here!" Immediately after hearing his tone, I pretended not to hear him, turned around, and started walking away with much haste. However, he raised his voice and in a more commanding tone said, "You hear me, young man? I said, come here!"

I became very nervous and started wondering if I had done something wrong. I am quite sure that my fear was attributed to my childhood experiences, especially those I had while living with my former foster parents. Anyway, I made a U-turn and started walking toward him. As soon as

---

provided both in the workplace and through technical vocational and education training (TVET) institutions. More information regarding the HEART Trust is available at http://jamaicadiasporaconnect.com/civicrm/profile/view?reset=1&id=88&gid=17, https://www.heart-nta.org/.

Chapter 5

I approached him, he said, "Young man, there is a human resource training school being built at Runaway Bay, and I would like for you to take this form and fill it out." I took the form, but instead of filling it out and mailing it off as per the instructions, I took it home and placed it in my chester draw, not realizing that this form was the key to unlock my future potential. Financial constraints were the main reason why I was a bit hesitant to consider any plans to further my academic or professional career. In fact, I was considering getting a job as an apprentice electrician after graduation so that I could help Aunt Lucy with the basic household expenses.

However, history has a way of repeating itself and, in my situation, it was quite apparent based on a recurring event. Approximately two weeks before graduation, I was once again walking along the same corridor, going about my business when, all of a sudden, I ran into Mr. Levy for the second time. Surely there was no escaping him because he was coming in the opposite direction. Immediately, it dawned on me that I had not filled out and mailed off the application to the HEART Trust as he had instructed me. I was hoping that he had long forgotten about what had transpired some two and a half months earlier.

With that said, I kept on walking as if we had no prior conversation regarding anything whatsoever. However, I was wrong about Mr. Levy. Either he cared deeply about my future academic and career advancement, or he simply had a memory like an elephant, or both. As he approached me, he said sternly, "Young man! Did you fill out the application form and mail it as I told you to?" Before I could answer, he went off into the Jamaican dialect and said, "Remember, dis is a big opportunity. Yuh can stay deh an waste it, yuh hear young man! It's all up to you, young man!" ("Remember this is an important opportunity. You can stay there and waste it away! It's all up to you!") I am not sure exactly how I replied or what I said, but what I do remember is that as soon as I got home that evening, I took the application form from the chester draw, filled it out, and mailed it off.

Even to this very day, I keep asking myself, why me? Why would Mr. Levy have gone out of his way to care so deeply about my future when there were hundreds of other students attending the school? It was not as if he'd been standing outside his office with a stack of forms handing them out to the students. In fact, I do not recall seeing him handing out any forms or chasing after any other students the day he presented me with the application form. From that day forward, that was the last encounter I had with Mr. Levy.

As for the Runaway Bay HEART Academy, I was not too optimistic, because I did not think that I had the intellect or the financial means necessary to become a trainee of this prestigious institution. Once again, I went on with my life with not much to look forward to (academically) beyond Albert Secondary School. However, there was always a little voice in my head that kept reminding me that all things are possible with God.

After graduation, I stayed at home, tending to the field and my small vegetable gardens. However, the entire process was interrupted one day when Aunt Lucy joined me at the table and said, "Desmond, we need to talk." She paused for a couple of seconds, then continued, "Desmond, I am not pleased with yuh just sitting down at home. Yuh hear mi, man? I am just not pleased with that. I know that

Chapter 5

this is a farming district and everyone does farming for a living, but I know you can go to school because I can see it in you." At that moment, I was not sure what message Aunt Lucy was trying to convey or what she was implying, so I just sat there and extended my listening ears. She concluded by saying, "I am going to call Leighton and have him take you to Kingston so that you can learn a trade." I am not sure how I responded to her proposal, but I came to realize that the Lord had even greater plans for me than the one Aunt Lucy was proposing.

Before Aunt Lucy could follow through with her plan, I was contacted by the HEART Trust via a letter instructing me to go to St. Ann's Bay (the capital of the parish of St. Ann) the following Saturday to sit an entrance exam. This entrance exam would determine if I had the required academic qualifications to become a trainee of the Runaway Bay HEART Academy. I was very excited about this opportunity because attending the HEART Academy would allow me to acquire a higher level of education and real-world career development training. Not only that, but an opportunity such as this would allow me to be a lot closer to home than if I had to migrate to Kingston. Anyway, the days went by quickly, and before I knew it, Friday arrived. It was the day before the big exam, which I had not yet prepped for. Seeing that I had no idea what the exam entailed, I decided to just go to bed and hope for the best. Despite being overwhelmed with anxiety and excitement, I did manage to get a good night's rest.

I got up very early Saturday morning, showered, dressed, and went straight to the dining room where Aunt Lucy had a delicious breakfast waiting for me. I was too anxious to eat, so I drank only a cup of hot chocolate. In a calm and comforting tone, Aunt Lucy said, "Desmond, don't yuh worry about a ting, just leave everything to the Lord. The Lord will do anything if you just put your hope and trust in him. Yuh hear mi man, anything." I did not have to say a word to Aunt Lucy because she noticed that I was looking quite worried regarding the whole outcome; thus, the reason for her little pep talk.

Shortly after that, I went by the roadway and waited for the bus to arrive. Within ten to fifteen minutes, the distinct noise from the Confidence bus horn came echoing through the mountains. Seeing that it was Saturday, one of the busiest days of the week, I was not so lucky as to find an empty seat. The bus was packed beyond capacity with passengers and all sorts of food produce. I had no other choice but to stand in a tight, sardine-like space while holding onto the overhead rails and rubbing shoulders with the other standing passengers.

After a couple of transfers and a "thousand" stops along the way, I finally arrived at St. Ann's Bay. I went directly to the community center, where the exam was scheduled to take place. I noticed that Lyndon, one of my former classmates, mentor, and friend from Albert Town Secondary School, was also there to sit the entrance exam. The entrance exam was a prerequisite for all those who wished to attend the HEART Academy. We were very early, so we camped out on the community grounds and made ourselves comfortable while catching up on our "old" school days. Later on, I saw other potential trainees arriving. I would estimate that there were approximately three hundred applicants present. Later that morning, we were summoned into the building and told to take seats.

Chapter 5

Shortly after that, we were presented with a welcome and good luck pep talk before commencing the exam.

After we were through with the exam, a well-dressed young man went up to the podium and introduced himself as Hugh Wint, the general manager of the Runaway Bay HEART Academy and Country Club. I do not recall everything he said, but I remember that he emphasized that thousands of applicants nationwide were vying for the two hundred available vacancies, and that only the best and the brightest would be chosen. After hearing those words, I started doubting my chances, because I had no idea how I had done on the exam. In fact, every question on the exam was a blur except for the one that asked, "What does the JTB abbreviation represent?" This question was easy because I have heard the JTB acronym many times on the radio. I believe the actual phrase was, "Brought to you by JTB, the Jamaica Tourist Board."

Although it was quite early in the afternoon, Lyndon and I decided to go home before the rush hour traffic. While we were on our way to the bus stop, I could not resist expressing my fear of the outcome to Lyndon. I remember saying to him, "Lyndon, do you think we stand a chance because of the number of people who applied?" Instead of concurring, Lyndon looked directly at me and said, "Desmond, no need to worry because the Lord has reserved two spots for us. Believe what I am telling you." Lyndon spoke as though he had gotten a glimpse into the future and had foreseen the outcome. Although I knew that Lyndon was always a person who exhibited a positive outlook on life, I am entirely convinced that what he said on that day was undoubtedly a divine intervention from the Lord.

What's Next

Before I bring this section to a close, I would like to share a little more with you concerning my friend Lyndon. Lyndon was also a very studious person and one who regarded time as the most precious gift. I remember one day while all of the students, including me, were clowning around in class, Lyndon intervened, looked directly at me, and said, "Desmond, just remember that in the end we all will be going our separate ways and the only thing that we can take with us is what is in our heads." What Lyndon was saying is that school is very important, and we should treat it as such because, after graduation, we will not have the privilege of taking our teachers or our friends with us as we embark on the next phase of life's journey. Now you know why everyone addressed him as Proff/Proffie. Once again, he had positive words of encouragement for me. His optimistic approach certainly provided me with a boost of confidence and I decided to leave everything in the hands of the Lord.

Let's Wait a Little While Longer

After several weeks had gone by with no feedback from the HEART Trust, Aunt Lucy decided that it was time to move ahead with Plan B. She sent a message to Leighton notifying him that he should come by and take me to Kingston so that I could start learning a trade. Once again, the process was interrupted when I received a telegram from the post office. The telegram was from the HEART Trust, requesting me to report to the Runaway Bay HEART Academy for an in-person interview. I was very excited! I was jumping up and down for joy.

I was not fond of commuting to Kingston because it was simply too far away from home, not to mention the

Chapter 5

poor road conditions. Just like clockwork, Leighton came by that same Friday to take me to Kingston. As soon as he got out of the car, he said, "Sir, are you ready? Do you have all your things packed?" With no hesitation, I told him that I had been summoned to the HEART Academy for an in-person interview and would not be accompanying him to Kingston that day. Once again, an outcome such as this is according to the will of God and not ours.

The following morning (Saturday), I got up, showered, dressed, and proceeded to the dining room. Aunt Lucy presented me with breakfast, but I was too anxious to eat, although I had a couple sips of the hot chocolate. Aunt Lucy comforted me with yet another hopeful reminder but she did so in plain English. She said, "Desmond, I want you to listen to me, man. Don't you worry about a thing, you hear mi man. Because when the Lord has something for you, it is for you and no one can take it away from you. You hear mi, man?" Once again, I knew that Aunt Lucy was doing her best to remind me that God was in control. Now that Aunt Lucy had instilled hope and confidence in me, it was time for me to face the next phase of the recruitment process.

Upon arrival at the Runaway Bay HEART Academy, I noticed that my friend Lyndon was right there with me. He was happy to see me and after greeting each other, we checked in with the security guard, who provided us with the instructions and directions to the building where the screening process was scheduled to take place. We went to the building and sat in the waiting area until it was our turn to be interviewed. Mr. Richards, the person who interviewed me, was quite familiar with my district (Sawyers). Not only that, but he knew my foster mother. The small talk that Mr. Richard and I had was the icebreaker I needed to quell the anxiety that was plaguing me. After the conclusion of the screening process, I was feeling very optimistic regarding the outcome. I also remembered what Aunt Lucy and Lyndon had told me regarding hope and optimism. Around the second or third week after the screening process, I received another telegram from the HEART Trust instructing me to report to the academy no later than the following Saturday to commence the one-year hotel management training program. The telegram also informed me to report to the academy to pick up my uniform material before the start of my training. I had no way of contacting Lyndon, which meant that I had no idea if he were also one of the "chosen ones." Later that week, Aunt Lucy received a message from Lyndon's aunt, and sure enough, it was good news. Lyndon had it right when he told me that I should not worry about the outcome because God had secured two of the available vacancies at the Runaway Bay HEART Academy for us.

I can assure you that this was one of the happiest days of my life, especially knowing that I was about to receive training at no direct cost to me. That is, I did not have to worry about tuition, boarding, or any other related costs. Wow! This opportunity was undoubtedly a miracle. The only thing that I said then, and the only thing I can say now, is that God does work in mysterious ways.

Monday morning, bright and early, I got up, dressed, and ate my breakfast in a cool, calm, and collected manner. Although I was experiencing mixed feelings regarding leaving home, deep down I was not at all worried. This time around, I did not receive any "do not worry" pep talks from Aunt Lucy. Presumably, she had seen the joy

Chapter 5

that was radiating all over my face. After breakfast, Aunt Lucy wished me safe travel, and I boarded the Confidence bus and commenced my journey to Runaway Bay.

Once again, after several transfers, I arrived at the HEART Academy. I went to the administration building, where I was presented with the uniform material and a list of the things that I needed to bring with me to the yearlong hotel management training. Money was a factor because I had just used up most of my savings to restock my vegetable inventory and for my graduation expenses. With that said, I was now in need of a little financial support to purchase the required items for the yearlong residential training. The uniform material was provided to the trainees free of cost; therefore, all I needed to do was to take the material to a tailor and have the pants and shirts made. Correction! I should have said, to have the pants tailored because the shirts were . . .

Okay, before I proceed any further, here is the not-so-pleasant but dramatic uniform shirt episode: As soon as I got home, I took the uniform material to Sonny (well, it was more like Sunny because I was about to "get burned") to have him tailor two white shirts and two pairs of navy blue pants, in accordance with the HEART Academy's uniform code. Within two days Sonny was through tailoring the two pairs of pants. He did a masterful job with the pants. He was still working on the shirts, but he assured me that he would have them ready by the following day. I stressed the importance of having the shirts completed on time, because I had to report for training no later than Saturday of that week. I also made it known to Sonny that I would not be allowed to attend training without the proper uniform. With that in mind, I visited Sonny

What's Next

Thursday morning of that week to see how he was doing. He assured me that he would have the shirts completed by Friday. I reminded him that I had to report for training no later than Saturday. Once again, he assured me that he would have the shirts ready by Friday evening.

By this time, Aunt Lucy had pretty much exhausted her funds, and I needed financial help to purchase the other items associated with the training. After going over all my available options, I decided that my last resort was to turn to the CDA. With that said, I went to the CDA office and pleaded my case to Ms. Davis, my presiding officer. With no hesitation, she put a process in motion and provided me with the necessary financial assistance to purchase most of the required items.

Friday morning of that week, I went to the store and purchased the required items I needed for the one-year room and board. I was delighted to have some new clothes to commence my training. However, something deep down within me kept reminding me that Sonny was not going to have the shirts ready when I showed up later that afternoon. After some six hours had gone by, I went back to see if Sonny had completed the shirts.

The minute I showed up, he handed me the shirts. My first reaction was, "Wow! Sonny came through!" Well, not so fast. The minute I looked at the shirts, I knew that something was not right. Nonetheless, I went ahead and tried on one and, immediately, the most obvious jumped right out at me. Instead of having a breast pocket, the shirt had what I would describe as an "Under Armour Pocket". Okay a little wittiness on my part but the truth is, the pockets on both shirts were located directly under the armpit. If you think that sewing the breast pockets under

Chapter 5

the armpit was the only thing that Sonny had messed up, then I say to you, think again! Instead of having two side seams like normal shirts, Sonny had one seam running directly down the back of the shirt. The collars on both shirts were completely messed up as well; they were sticking out like rabbit ears. Both shirts were seriously messed up! In the words of an angry American, "Sonny screwed up big time!"

I am here to assure you that the above episode is true and verifiable. I mean, I did not have to add any drama to this episode because it was pure drama in, of, and by itself. I was very disappointed with Sonny for not being honest with me. He should have told me from the beginning that he did not know how to tailor a shirt. And would you believe that Sonny dared to tell me that he was not going to charge me for the shirts! Not only that, but he made no mention of how and when he would reimburse me for the material. Note to self, "Never pay a tailor in advance." Today I can make light of the situation, but back then it was a bit frustrating because I had no uniform shirts and no money, and the day to check into the academy was fast approaching. Nonetheless, I was very happy to be leaving for training, so I decided to take my loss and move on. Furthermore, that would be the last time I did any business with Sonny.

I went home and told Aunt Lucy what had happened and she was very upset as well. Now I was left with no money to replace the uniform material or the shirts. Faced with such a dilemma, Aunt Lucy and I decided to put "one and one" together and see what alternative we could come up with. I managed to find a white shirt that was badly worn out but, with no other option, I had to make do.

What's Next

However, I was still in need of at least one more shirt. And that was when Aunt Lucy went into her closet and searched through every rack of clothes until she found a blouse that resembled a shirt except that it had a little embroidery located in the center of the breast pocket. She gave it to me, and with no hesitation, I packed it away in my bag and went to bed.

I did not sleep well that night because I was very anxious but at the same time overwhelmed with joy, knowing that I was about to embark on yet another new and exciting academic frontier. Finally, the long night passed, and it was Saturday, the dawn of a new era. I woke up very early, but never early enough because Aunt Lucy was already in the kitchen preparing breakfast. I could see the joy radiating from her face as well. She greeted me with a big and pleasant good morning, and I replied likewise. After breakfast, I had a long talk with Aunt Lucy. It was quite emotional for me to be leaving home, not knowing when I would return. However, our conversation ended because I heard the Confidence bus horn echoing through the mountains. I said one final goodbye to Aunt Lucy and Sister Lin then I went by the roadway.

As the bus arrived I waved my hand vigorously, because this was surely not the day I wanted to find myself being left behind. In Jamaica, even if you are at the bus stop or roadway, you must signal to the bus driver or taxi operator with a hand gesture because if you forget, then you will certainly be left behind choking on carbon dioxide. That morning, the bus driver saw my hand gesture and stopped the bus. I *hurried* on board but had to stand because the bus was packed with passengers. Notice how I emphasized the word "hurried." I did so because, on

Chapter 5

several occasions, the conductor or the passengers would say, "Hole aan deh driva!" ("Hold on or please wait for a minute driver!") This reaction was necessary because the driver tended to drive off before the passengers were through boarding the bus.

CHAPTER 6

KNOWLEDGE FROM THE HEART

As I was on my way to the Runaway Bay HEART Academy, I found myself reminiscing on the two and a half years I had spent with my chosen foster mother, Aunt Lucy. My expectation had been for her to provide me with life's essentials, such as food, clothes, and shelter, in exchange for the manual labor I could provide her. Having such a premise at the forefront of my mind, I never dreamt that I would one day be leaving home to embark on a new and exciting career opportunity such as this one. As I stood there holding onto the overhead rails, I simply could not come to terms with the rapid transformation that was taking place right before my eyes. What I had once perceived to be far beyond my reach had become a reality.

When I arrived at the HEART Academy, the security guard greeted me at the entrance and asked if I was one of the resident trainees, to which I replied with a resounding, "Yes, I am." I do not recall how the rest of the verification process went because I was overwhelmed to the point that I found myself being taken up with the beautiful landscape and buildings.

Chapter 6

All the information you need to know about HEART. Please shove the palm leaves out of the way to access the phone numbers. Okay that might be a bit difficult so here you go... 876-973-6671-4, 876-973-4027

I was very fortunate to be one of the first resident trainees to be attending such a prestigious academy. Undoubtedly, this was a grand opportunity for me, especially knowing that it would not have been feasible for Aunt Lucy to finance this or similar training on my behalf. It was hard to believe that the training I was about to receive was at no direct cost to me. This training institution was a golden opportunity that exceeded my wildest imagination. I could go on and on expressing the way I felt, but I need to proceed because there are a lot more training events to cover.

After clearing security, I was directed to the main auditorium for the next onboarding process. Mr. Wint, the general manager, and Ms. Stimpson, the manager of the academic sector, welcomed us to the Runaway Bay HEART Academy and outlined the agenda for the upcoming training period. Mr. Wint stressed the importance of the institution so that we would realize that this was a once-in-a-lifetime opportunity that should not be taken lightly. After he was through, Ms. Stimpson picked up where he left off. She emphasized what was required of us academically and highlighted the rules and regulations, which were very few seeing that we were the first batch of resident trainees. She concluded by wishing everyone success throughout the program.

This is the view of the original section of the Runaway Bay Hotel, today is known as the Cardiff Hall Hotel & Spa.

A glimpse of the newly added section of the Cardiff Hall Hotel & Spa.

Chapter 6

After the welcoming session was completed, one of the administrative staff members commenced the roll call. She read the names of each trainee along with his or her assigned dormitory. As their names were read, the trainees would take their luggage and proceed to their assigned dorms. After several names were announced, I finally heard mine along with the assigned dorm, which was number six. The minute I got to the dorm, I placed my luggage, two small bags, on one of the top bunk beds that were located at the very end, furthest away from the entrance of the dorm.

With no hesitation, I started packing away my belongings into the locker that was closest to the top bunk. While I was unpacking, one of the trainees, Harrington, approached me and, in a rather deep and crude tone of voice, said, "Small youth, I would like to have the top bunk, see!" With no hesitation and zero resistance, I took my things off the top bunk, placed them on the bottom bunk, and affirmed that the bottom bunk was what I had in mind. I was quite nervous to the point that I told him that I had only placed my bags on the top bunk but had no intention of occupying it. Yeah right! Who am I kidding? I had every intention of occupying the top bunk. However, I had heard too many horror stories concerning boarding school, so this was not the time and place for me to start resisting someone who was twice my body mass and had a voice so rough it could scrape the paint off the walls. Okay, I went overboard with my analysis, but I know you get the point that Harry scared the daylights out of me. Not only did I surrender to his demand, but from that point forward, I was addressed as "Small Boy/Small Youth," both by my fellow trainees and the faculty and

I used to occupy the left bottom bunk, and Harry the top bunk.

staff members. I was never able to get rid of that pet name. However, giving up the top bunk and being addressed as "Small Boy" was indeed a small price to pay, because I was not going to let anything get in the way of this wonderful opportunity.

Here is a little look-ahead regarding this top-bunk episode. Shortly after this incident, I found Harry to be one of the most pleasant and thoughtful trainees at the academy. And the rough vocal tone he had used on me that day was just an act. Anyway, it worked because he scared me into submission right away.

After all of the trainees were assigned to their respective dorms and had finished unpacking their belongings, a number of the trainees started conversing among themselves, because there was not much else for us to do. I did not know anyone in my dorm, so I just sat there and kept really quiet while waiting for the next event to unfold.

Chapter 6

Moreover, I had just received an early dose of "roughed up," so it was quite advantageous for me to sit quietly in my little space on the bottom bunk.

Later that evening, I heard a loud voice and a barrage of clapping echoing from the balcony of the cafeteria. It was one of the cafeteria staff members. She kept repeating, "Students, it's supper time. Students, it's supper time . . ." I remember nobody wanted to be the first to leave the dorm. Probably nobody wanted to give others the impression that he or she was the greedy one, or as we say in Jamaica, the "craben" or "wanga-gut" person. However, that was not true for Harry. After witnessing that nobody wanted to be the first to make a move, he jumped down from his top bunk and said, "I don't know about you guys, but I am starving." Just as Harry stepped out of the dorm and was on his way to the cafeteria, the rest of us, including the trainees from the other dorms, followed suit. All we needed was to have someone assume the role of "the leader of the pack."

Now you know that this theory holds true in both the human and the animal kingdoms. As soon as we reached the cafeteria, each of us took a tray from the stack and joined the queue. When I got close enough to see what was on the menu, I was overwhelmed. It looks more like an all-inclusive resort buffet rather than an academy cafeteria. I believe there were fish, oxtail, and lots of vegetable on the menu. Well, who needs to keep track when all the choices looked so delicious? Oops, I almost forgot the thirst-quenching, homemade fruit punch. That day I enjoyed every bit of my first "five-star" meal.

After supper, we dispersed to our various dorms and sort of camped out there for the rest of the evening. My friend Lyndon (he was assigned to dorm 7) and I shared a few memorable recollections while we watched a movie. We made a pact with each other that we would take full advantage of this once-in-a-lifetime opportunity. We also reminisced about the years we had spent at Albert Town Secondary. At approximately 10:00 p.m., we all retired to our beds because we were tired from the long day's activities.

Throughout the first couple of days, we spent most of our time getting to know each other because we had been selected from different parishes across the island. However, within a couple of weeks, small clusters of trainees with shared interests began popping up throughout the academy. The dormitory accommodation reminded me of my orphanage days. The dorms were designed to accommodate sixteen trainees, however, for the first three months, I believe there were only ten or eleven trainees in my dorm.

My first night at this academy is one that I will always remember. As I lay in my bottom bunk, I was filled with mixed emotions. I was thinking about how fortunate I was to have been given such a wonderful opportunity. It was more than a miracle for me to have been chosen from approximately four thousand applicants nationwide. Despite knowing that with God, all things are possible, at times I found myself second-guessing my ability to complete the training successfully. Not only was I up due to anxiety and the overwhelming mixed emotions, but the bright lights that were strung across the property were also a factor. Living in the country for my entire life meant that I was not accustomed to this much excitement.

Chapter 6

Anyway, after much reminiscing, I finally fell asleep. Before I knew it, the night was gone and it was daylight once more. Although I did not have to report to training, I got up early and showered to avoid the rush. The shower was a soothing one because the facility also provided us with hot water. After I was through showering, I went back to the dorm and sat on my bed, using the time to prepare my mind and body for the yearlong training. My thought process was interrupted at approximately 7:00 a.m., when everyone got out of bed and started moving about, except for Harry. He was the sleeping dog that everyone knew not to disturb. Harry cared dearly about two things, his food and his sleep. Everyone got the message very early that nobody messed with Harry's food or disturbed his sleep. On several occasions, the dorm monitor had to knock several times on Harry's bed to let him know that it was time for him to wake up. As for me, I was always an early bird, which never sat too well with Harry. Several mornings Harry would say to me in a jovial manner, "Small Youth, what's up with this getting up early in the morning and making all that noise?"

How did the second day's events unfold? After taking a shower, everyone (except for Harry) made their beds and sort of camped out in their respective dorms while waiting for the breakfast signal. Harry was one of the trainees who did not shower before breakfast. His philosophy was that a hungry man does not have the energy to take a shower or move about. One of his more comical phrases was, "It is more likely for a hungry man to pass out in the shower than it is for a man with a full stomach." Somewhere around 7:30 a.m., we got the signal we had been waiting for. It was time for us to go to the cafeteria for breakfast.

Despite receiving the "breakfast is ready" signal, nobody wanted to be the first person to walk out the door. Once again, that was not true for Harry because he jumped down from his bed and said, "I have not eaten since yesterday, and I am starving. I don't know why you guys are afraid of food." Shortly after that, everyone followed suit.

If my memory serves me well, the breakfast menu choices were ackee and codfish[9] (dried salted cod), corned beef, cabbage with sliced bread, and boiled green banana. Hot chocolate (or cocoa tea, as per Jamaicans) was served with our breakfast. This surely was a very good beginning because, so far, the HEART Academy certainly negated all the horror stories I had heard concerning boarding school. Besides, the meal experience was far different from the ones I had while living at the orphanage (mostly dried bulgur). Once again, I enjoyed my five-star meal gracefully.

After breakfast, I went back to the dorm and kept busy doing little things such as organizing my locker, packing my bookbag, and just about any other school-related activity that would keep me busy. After I was through, and with not much else to do, I sat on my bed and observed the other trainees as they made their way in and out of the dorm.

It was time for lunch, and the procedure was pretty much the same as breakfast, except that lunch was the traditional Jamaican Sunday meal. Our first Sunday meal was rice and peas (red beans), baked chicken, fried fish, vegetable, and fruit punch. After we were through with the delicious and filling lunch, we watched television for a while. As for me, I had no knowledge regarding

---

9 By the way, ackee and codfish is the Jamaican national dish.

Chapter 6

the programs that were being broadcast. Aunt Lucy had not owned a television, so I had not watched any television programming in approximately three years. At the academy, we received our television service via the dish-network, which meant we had HBO, Cinemax, and many more channels. I was only watching television because we had not yet officially commenced our training. As soon as the training process got underway, I placed television watching on the back burner. Well, it was more like taking it entirely off the stove. Finally, after approximately six hours, it was time to go to the dining room for supper. Once again, we followed the same procedure. That is, we ate supper, went back to the dorm, and watched television until approximately 10:00 p.m. before retiring to bed.

No More Delay, Let the Training Begin

The training was scheduled to begin Monday morning, so bright and early (somewhere around 6:30 a.m.), I got up, showered, dressed, and waited for the "breakfast is served" signal. After breakfast, we went back to the dorm, and those who had not yet showered or dressed in their uniforms did so. After waiting for a good fifteen to twenty minutes, we went to the auditorium for the morning's devotion. The auditorium served as a multipurpose room that was used for dining, devotion, and entertainment. It was a beautiful sight to see the girls wearing their white blouses and light blue skirts and the boys wearing their navy-blue pants and white shirts. Oops, did I say all the boys were in their white shirts? That statement is 99 percent accurate, because I was the only male trainee who was wearing a white blouse. I was quite lucky that nobody knew the difference, except for a small number of trainees who were fascinated by the little embroidery on the breast pocket; which they thought was unique. Can you imagine what would have happened if I had been wearing a pair of female shoes to complement my blouse? Okay, let's move on because there is no need for us to speculate.

The managers, Mr. Wint and Ms. Stimpson, attended our first morning's devotion. Just a reminder, in Jamaica there is no real separation of state and church. Therefore, everyone--Jews, Gentiles, and Rastafarians--attended the morning's devotion because, in Jamaica, race and religious affiliation are considered insignificant in this and other similar settings. For our first devotion, we sang songs and read scripture verses from the Bible, followed by a closing prayer. After the devotion, Mr. Wint and Ms. Stimpson welcomed us to the academy and outlined the rules and procedures that were expected of us. This was done a second time so as to accommodate the trainees who were not present the first day. We were also introduced to the faculty members. Finally, we dispersed to our vocational training areas.

I had chosen Hotel Engineering--heating and cooling (HVAC), electrical, and plumbing--and Landscape Horticulture as my areas of interest, therefore, I proceeded directly to that vocational training area. Upon arrival, we were greeted by Mr. Clarke, the engineer manager; Mr. Mills, the landscape and horticulture manager; Mr. Fisher, the electrical engineer supervisor; and Mr. McFarlin (Mr. Mac), the plumber. After introductions, the next two hours were allocated to academic learning. Throughout the initial stage, Mr. Clarke and Mr. Fisher assumed the responsibility for the academic portion of the training.

Chapter 6

However, within a couple of weeks, the role of the academic training was transitioned to a full-time instructor, Mr. Archer.

Later that morning, Mr. Clarke went over the academic portion of the Hotel Engineering program. Around noon, we were dismissed for lunch, after which we attended the math and English language sessions, which were taught by Mr. Thorpe and Ms. Brown, respectively. The rest of the afternoon was left up to each vocational area instructor for practical training. However, seeing that it was quite early in training, we did not participate in any practical training for the first two to three weeks. Throughout such time, we participated in additional in-class academic training.

After we were through with the academic training for the day, we went back to the dorm and relaxed while waiting for supper. After supper we showered, then a number of us camped out in the dorm and continued our "getting to know you" sessions, while the others watched television. Finally, we retired to bed around 10:00 p.m. I was very pleased with every aspect of the training thus far. As for the rest of the week's training, the routine was quite similar to that of the first day.

We quickly became used to the routine of a typical week at the academy. A typical week at the HEART Academy included a number of routine activities: At approximately 7:00 a.m., the dorm monitor would bang several times on the dorm windows signaling to the trainees that it was time to wake up. I remember the dorm monitor would repeat his favorite "Rise and shine" wake-up ritual to get the attention of the trainees who were still sleeping. And, as we all knew, Harry was always one of those trainees whom the dorm monitor had to provide with a personal "rise and shine" wake-up ritual. Next we dress in our exercise attire and go through a workout drill, if one was scheduled by the dorm monitor. This drill was much despised by many of the trainees because we had to get up early and run approximately two miles. For me, however, this was a no-sweat, piece of cupcake, because I was accustomed to jogging some seven miles to and from school each day while living with my former foster parents and approximately eight miles from school while living with Aunt Lucy.

After the morning exercise, we would complete our assigned chores, which included dorm and cafeteria duties. The trainees who were not assigned to any morning duties would shower and dress in their uniforms or work attire, per their respective classes or hotel practical training program. After breakfast we attended the morning's devotion and then headed off to the academic portion of the training.

After lunch, we had a break, during which we could relax in the dorm for twenty-five to thirty minutes. Then those of us who were assigned to practical training would proceed to the hotel. This step in the daily process was contingent upon the instructors and the prospective managers associated with the different training programs. For example, the trainees majoring in Food and Beverage Preparation would proceed to the hotel and assist with the preparation and serving of the meals. Reservationists, Accounting, and Merchandising would assist with the bookings, bookkeeping, and purchasing duties. Housekeeping would assist with the cleaning of the rooms and laundry-related activities. As for the Hotel Engineer/ Maintenance trainees, we would ensure that all the hotel

Chapter 6

equipment, electrical, landscape, heating and cooling, and plumbing systems were in working order and were properly maintained. The trainees who were not assigned to any afternoon practical or academic training would indulge in other activities, such as doing their laundry, participating in sports, watching television, or, like me, burning every possible free hour studying.

Supper was served at 6:00 p.m., after which we would shower. Around 8:00 p.m. we would go to the library or the open auditorium and study for two hours. When the long day's activities came to an end, somewhere between 10:00 or 10:30 p.m., we would finally retire to bed.

From that point forward, things were pretty much standard except for the practical training. Each trainee had to go through a cross-training, hands-on program that included all aspects of the Hotel Management program. That is, although I specialized in Hotel Engineering and Landscape Horticulture, I also had to spend time in Housekeeping, Food Preparation, Waiting and Bar Tending, Accounting, Inventory Control, and Front Desk Reservations. We were also given the opportunity to spend anywhere from four to six weeks at another hotel or company for additional practical training. I completed my off-site practical training with Econergy Engineering, which gave me the opportunity to work on major projects at several hotels located throughout the Montego Bay area.

Faith Based Journey

Although I was quite busy with my hotel management training, I decided to take some time out of my busy schedule to complete a significant phase of my faith journey. With that said, I took a weekend off, went home, and discussed with Aunt Lucy my desire to be baptized. With no hesitation, she said, "Desmond, if this is your heart's desire, then I will go ahead and make the necessary arrangements with Brother Sommers for you." After several short but meaningful counseling sessions with the pastor, he scheduled a date for my baptism ceremony.

On the day of my baptism, two unexpected occurrences happened to me, which reminded me that I must always forgive those who trespass against me, regardless. The first came when I found out that the baptismal ceremony was scheduled to take place in another branch of the Gospel Chapel instead of our usual church building. This was certainly not a problem because this was my heart's desire, and I wanted to follow through irrespective of where the baptismal ceremony was scheduled to take place. However, on the day of the ceremony, as I sat there in the church going through my final mental preparations, I heard the pastor announce that the actual baptismal ceremony was going to be carried out by John the Baptist. Okay, John the Baptist was not the person announced by the pastor; but instead, it was my former foster father. The announcement became even more apparent when I looked up and saw him in the pool. My first reaction was, "Why is he in the pool! I need to get out of here because I may never get out of the water alive!" Okay, I am just kidding about the need to get out of the church. Although I was a bit surprised, I can assure you that those thoughts never crossed my mind because the grace of God has taught me to forgive my former foster parents.

Besides, I realized that my relationship with God is not contingent upon a person, a system, or a nation. Or any worldly thing, for that matter. The fellowship I enjoy with my Lord and savior transcends the ones I experienced with my fellow humankind. Therefore, the actions of my former foster parents did not negate or diminish the love and compassion of God that they professed through their preaching, teaching, or singing. In other words, irrespective of the messenger, the word of God is true, and it is indispensable. I would like to encourage you not to let the actions of a person, system, or nation cause you to walk away from the undeserved love, grace, and mercy of God. Despite the minor distraction, the baptismal service went well.

Reuniting with my Former Foster Parents Adopted Daughter

At the beginning of the sixth month, the academy enrolled another batch of trainees and, to my surprise, my former foster mother's adopted daughter (Joy) was also one of the trainees. She was there to complete a six-month Food and Beverage program. This was a wonderful opportunity for me because she was also boarding at the academy and we had plenty of time to reminisce on the good and not-so-good days. She and her son, Christopher, and Michael her adopted brother was still living at home with their parents (my former foster parents). Her mother was still a teacher but her father was not employed because he was no longer working for the bauxite company. We also fill each other in on other important aspects of our lives.

Academic Turbulence

Things were not all smooth sailing for me because I was struggling to keep up academically. I found it quite challenging to retain the required information due to the current study environment. That is, there were limited study areas available for the trainees to complete their assignments and to study for upcoming exams. The other drawback was that we had only two to three hours' study time, which was certainly not sufficient for me to get all my studies done.

Moreover, the study environment was way too noisy for me to concentrate on my studies. Besides, I needed three or four times the allotted study hours to be successful academically. With that said, I pleaded my case to the academic manager, Ms. Stimpson. After listening to my rationale, she permitted me to use the engineering/maintenance classroom as my designated study area. Although I did not fill her in on the main reason why I needed more time to study, I did promise her that if given more time, then I would certainly improve academically.

Not only did I take advantage of the extended study hours, but I also changed my study routine. Instead of studying with the other trainees, I would take an hour nap then I would go directly to the engineering classroom where I would study until 4:00 a.m., or sometimes until 6:00 a.m. I must admit that Ms. Stimpson had no idea that most of the time I was in the engineering room studying all night. However, the sacrifice paid off because, from that point forward, I made a significant improvement in my academic work, which was noticed and recognized by the faculty members.

Chapter 6

Here is the point that I would like to stress, mostly to students. A problem is not like vintage wine, it does not get better with the passage of time. Therefore, the moment that you recognize that something is not working, please do not sit there and convince yourself that it will get better if you just ignore it. If that is your premise, then you are merely prolonging the inevitable. As for me, I had to identify my weaknesses and act rather quickly to overcome them. Moreover, this was a once-in-a-lifetime opportunity that I refused to take lightly or take for granted.

The Unexplainable Intervention

I do have another divine intervention to share with you. However, before I do so, I will have to go back to the first two weeks of my training at the HEART Academy. One of the academy requirements was for each trainee to undergo a series of medical checkups by the district nurse. For me, this turned out to be much more than just a regular checkup, because I was about to cross paths with someone very special. I remember the very first afternoon the nurse came by the academy. At first, I was a bit reluctant to go through with the checkup because I was not too keen on the whole needle thing. It's like not wanting to go to the dentist or, as it was in my case, not wanting to shave my locks on my very first visit to the orphanage.[10] As the process commenced, I observed as the other trainees made their way into the room, got their checkups, and came back out alive. Not wanting to be seen as a wimp by my fellow

---

10 For context, please refer to volume 1.

trainees, I decided to just man up and go through with this mandatory health checkup.

With that in mind, I got up, walked to the building, up the stairs, and finally into the examination room. Before I could say hi, the nurse looked at me, knitted her brow, and said, "Do you know that I always wanted a son but was never blessed with one. If I did, he would look just like you." I stood there speechless for a brief moment because I was not sure how I should respond to such a compliment. There she was, a total stranger, whom I had never met before, informing me that I could be considered her son or the son she had always wanted. She either needed a new pair of glasses or needed to take a look in the mirror one more time because I am not sure if she really wanted an ugly person like me to be her son. Despite the added humor, I was quite honored to have gotten such a wonderful, life-changing compliment. I always see myself as an orphan child who had been told by my former foster mother never to address her or anyone else as mother, mummy, mommy, or any other label that would give the impression that such person was my mother. Anyway, after she was through with the examination process, I thanked her and walked out the door.

Now that I had gotten the scary health checkup and the "You could have been my son" compliment out of the way, it was time for me to settle down with my studies. However, before I could get too comfortable, I was once again summoned to the nurse's office for my second and final checkup. This time the process did not intimidate me. In fact, I was one of the first trainees to show up in the examination room. As soon as I entered the room, the nurse addressed me as her son. She said, "Hello, my son," and I replied with a simple, "Hello, nurse." I was not sure

Chapter 6

if I should address her as mom or mother because I could still hear my former foster mother's "Don't you dare address me as your mother" deafening remarks echoing in my ears.

After she was through with the checkup, she and I conversed for a short while because there were no other trainees in the waiting area. It was more of a "getting to know you" session. Although everyone in the district addressed her by her profession (Nurse), she told me that her name was Mrs. Laurel HoSang, and that she had four daughters and a husband, who worked for the St. Ann Parish Council. I told her about Aunt Lucy and how she had become my foster mother. Mrs. HoSang also said that she was very familiar with the district where my foster mother lived and that her husband used to pass by Aunt Lucy's home frequently while working for the Trelawny Parish Council. After conversing for a while, she asked me if I would like to stop by her home on the weekends because she lived within proximity to the academy. I thanked her for her generous offer, and that was where our conversation ended for that day.

Meeting My HEART Family

One Saturday afternoon, Mrs. HoSang contacted me and asked if I would like to come to her home and meet the rest of the family. Without any hesitation, I replied with a resounding, "Yes!" Within a matter of minutes, she came by and took me to her home. The minute I got out of the car and looked around, I thought I had been taken to a palace. The castle-shaped house and beautiful garden captivated my mind. However, before I got too carried away with the external beauty, she invited me inside and introduced me to the rest of the family. First, she introduced me to Cleopatra, known as Clair, her oldest daughter (actually, stepdaughter). I remember Clair said to me, "So you are mommy's little son that she keeps talking about." I am not sure what my reply was but after my brief meet and greet with Clair, Mrs. HoSang introduced me to her husband, Arthur, and the rest of her children: Desiree (Desie), Kimberly (Kim), and Yolanda. After the introductions, Mr. HoSang came over to where I was sitting and said, "So, I heard you are from the Trelawny area. Where in Trelawny are you from?" I said, "Sawyers," and told him that my foster mother Ms. Lucy Brady (Aunt Lucy) resided in the Burke district. He then replied, "Yes man, I know who you are talking about. It is the lady that has the little shop right by the main road in Burke. I used to stop by the little bar across the street on my way from work and have a drink."

Then it dawned on me that God surely controls destiny. Although I was meeting the HoSang family for the very first time, I felt as though we had a lot in common based on their humble beginnings. From that point forward, my visits started to feel a lot more like being at home rather than just another visit. I was very happy for this wonderful opportunity. Although I was away from home and Aunt Lucy, God had provided me with a family that was within proximity to the academy. From that point forward, I was invited to spend weekends and holidays with my newly found family. Mr. HoSang and I used to spend quite a bit of time talking about sports, mostly cricket. We did not only talk about sports, but we also spend some time discussing other general topics from the gentlemen's domain; something that I had not been privy to while living with my former foster parents.

Chapter 6

Academy Perks

At the academy, our time was not just consumed with work and study. In fact, the academy also supported other extracurricular activities, which included soccer and volleyball competitions. Occasionally, we were taken on field trips so that we could experience the managerial operations of other significant hotels. In addition, the academy would treat us to an occasional party or concert. Overall, we were treated very well. The academy maintained a very high standard, especially in the vocational training areas. In fact, several trainees were awarded supervisory roles throughout their initial full-time employment, while others were promoted to management roles shortly after being employed.

The Final Leg of the Journey

The training was going great! However, time flew by rather quickly and before we had a chance to clear our throats, graduation day was right around the corner. This graduation was going to be very special because the prime minister (the Honorable Edward Seaga), his entourage, and other high-profile dignitaries were scheduled to attend. It was like having the president of the United States as a guest speaker at your graduation ceremony. The Runaway Bay HEART Academy, from what I heard, was the prime minister's pet project. He regarded it very highly. In fact, he spent several weekends at the academy's Runaway Bay Hotel. Therefore, great emphasis was placed on our looking our best and conducting ourselves in a professional manner, which had been endorsed from the very first day of our training.

However, "looking our best" became a problem for me because I was unable to afford a suit. Once again, the goodness of God was about to manifest in a very special way. Shortly before graduation, Mrs. HoSang asked me if I had a suit for the occasion. Instead of just letting her know that I was unable to afford one, I told her that I had not yet decided what to wear. However, based on my response, she sensed that I was experiencing financial difficulties. The following day, she contacted me and told me to meet her at the security guard post. I did accordingly, and within a couple of minutes, I saw her white Sunbeam Hillman Hunter car (or Roots, as per Jamaicans) coming down the hill at full speed. She pulled over by the guard post, stretched her hand out the window, presented me with a handful of cash, and said, "Please go and get the material for your graduation suit." I thanked her many times, and she replied with the usual "not a problem" response and drove off.

Without further delay, I boarded a minivan and went directly to a little outlet store in Ocho Rios and purchased the material. As soon as I returned to the academy, Mrs. HoSang asked me if I had a tailor in mind. I told her I did not. That was a factual statement because this was undoubtedly not the time to have Sonny experiment with my suit. Okay, let's pause and think for a moment. Can you imagine if I had given Sonny the job of tailoring my suit? Well, let's give him credit because, within a couple of hours, he would have had the pair of pants fully tailored. However, even to this very day, I would still be waiting

Chapter 6

for the shirt, the jacket, and the vest. I would be the only trainee at the graduation looking like a topless Putin. Anyway, Mrs. HoSang took me to one of her tailors, and he tailored an elegant suit for me.

Now that I had my suit all tailored, I was more than ready for my graduation. At least that's what I thought, until the day of the ceremony, when I found out that I did not have a tie to go with the suit. Once again, I explained to Mrs. HoSang my need, and she said, "Desmond, come on over and look in Arthur's closet to see if you can find one that goes with the suit." I hurried over to her home and searched Mr. HoSang's closet until I found a tie that matched the suit perfectly. Oops, I should not use the words match and perfectly when referring to attire, because my wife would beg to differ. Nonetheless, I was now in tip-top shape for my first high-profile graduation.

Celebration Day

The day of the graduation finally arrived, and all of the trainees were dressed in their very best. I mean, we were dressed from head to toe. This graduation ceremony was the first of its kind to be held at the academy, and I can assure you that it was destined to be an unprecedented one. That day, it appeared as though the hours were placed in overdrive, and before I could grasp what was really happening, the graduation ceremony had already begun.

That evening, it was not just the trainees, but also the faculty and managers who were dressed in their very best. Aunt Lucy and a number of the church members were in attendance. I was delighted when I looked around and saw my foster mother and a number of my fellow church sisters and brothers in attendance. I was overjoyed because I had no idea that they were coming. My former foster mother also attended the graduation ceremony. She was there to support her adopted daughter, Joy, on her significant accomplishment as well.

It was very rewarding to know that the hard work and the sleepless nights had finally paid off. I was also honored to have received two awards for my outstanding academic achievements. The first award was for being the most outstanding Hotel Engineering/Maintenance trainee and the second for being the most improved trainee overall. I can assure you that walking across the stage twice to receive my awards made me feel as though I was a never-ending supernova. After receiving my second award, the Custos (the representative of the governor-general) of the parish of St. Ann, got up, shook my hand, and said, "You make us Tomlinsons very proud, and I am proud of you." His remarks highlighted the fact that his family name was also Tomlinson. The prime minister also congratulated me on my outstanding accomplishments. However, it is in moments like these that I think of my only brother and the fact that he was denied the opportunity to live out his dreams.

As I compiled my autobiography over the years, I have learned many things regarding my academic career. Although there is not enough time to elaborate on all of them, I would like to share one of the more important ones with you. Being the recipient of the most improved student award by Albert Town Secondary and the Runaway Bay HEART Academy made me realize that although each stage of my academic journey started out as a struggle, I was able to overcome my learning impediment through long and countless hours of studying.

Chapter 6

I believe firmly that this learning impediment came about from the environments to which my siblings and I were subjected. However, my academic outlook was changed when Aunt Lucy intervened in my life. Also being conscious of my limitations, I resorted to drastic measures such as studying long hours. Most of the time, I would be up studying all night. A number of my peers and professors inquired why I had to put forth so much effort academically. Although I did not provide them with any insight regarding my childhood, I believe they knew that I had to resort to such measures just to be successful academically.

Concerning learning, I am not an "out of the gate" speed learner; however, with perseverance and a strong determination to succeed, I managed to overcome. It was this personal trait that was noticed by the faculty and staff of Albert Town Secondary School and the Runaway Bay HEART Academy. To prove my point, I would like to provide you with a little academic humor that occurred many years later. Most (more like all) of the time, I would be the very last person to complete an exam, which was known to everyone, including my professors. In fact, the instructor who was assigned to proctor the exam that I was sitting would realize that he or she would have to be there for the entire duration. In fact, I would take every minute of the allotted time to complete the exam. At the final class exam, one of my professors Dr. Gordon, made an announcement asking the first person who completed the exam to drop off the end-of-term surveys at the administrative office. I was the first to volunteer for this task by raising my hand. With no hesitation, Dr. Gordon said, "Desmond, put your hand down, because you and I know that you are going to be the last person to leave the room this afternoon." And that was when the entire class cracked up laughing.

While I am on this topic, I might as well fill you in on another humor. After studying the same material for many days with no success (nothing would stick), I got a bit frustrated and started banging and scratching my head with my hands. At that very moment, while I was banging away at my head, my Jamaican roommate, Michael, came into the room and said, "Wait! Bwoy, a mad yuh a mad bwoy?" ("Boy, are you going crazy?") I was literally pounding the information into my head.

I can assure you that there were times when I felt the tears coming, because I was exhausted and felt as if I were about to pass out due to the overwhelming amount of effort, including sleepless nights, that was required for me to be successful academically. There were times when I felt like quitting, especially when I realized that I would have to go over the material another two or three times for it to register in my brain. Many years later, my slow learning was one of the factors that caused me to lose my first well paid, well sought-after job.[11] Irrespective of my learning impediment, I hope you had a good laugh because I believe it is a healthy dose of therapy to poke a little fun at your own weaknesses once in a while.

On a more solemn note, there were times when I would get upset and blame my parents, especially my father. However, I realized that such action only caused me more psychological pain. So here is the moral of my story, and one that I would like to relay to everyone,

---

11 If you are curious to know, please have a sneak peek at volume 4 of my autobiography.

especially the younger generation: Do not beat up on yourself or give up just because you are not the smartest or fastest learner among your peers. Nor should you be afraid to take on challenging roles because you may not succeed on your first or even on your second or third tries. So what if you have to spend an extra hour or two (or many more nights, as it was in my case) more than your peers to understand a topic or to study for an exam? So what if you have to take all the allotted time to complete an assignment or be the very last person to leave an examination room, as it was in my case? So what if your friends at times make fun of you or even go as far as to ridicule you because you have to study most of the time? So what and so what?

I am here to say none of that matters. What really matters is that at the end of the day you can say to yourself, I have given it my all and I have done my best. Always remember that the most important thing in life is for you to keep persevering and to keep measuring your progress by setting the bar a little higher each time. Here is a little motto I would like to share with you as it pertains to my learning approach: *What I was unable to get done in haste, I was able to get done at a slow but consistent pace.* And if at times you find yourself being overwhelmed like I was, then please recite Proverbs 2, verses 1 through 6, or other uplifting quotes from your favorite books or admired persons.

Life After Graduating

Now that the training was over and the graduation excitement had subsided, the real question for me was, "Where do I go from here?" Most of the trainees had packed their belongings and left for their respective homes, while others who had received jobs started to relocate to the nearby communities. I was still at the academy because I had not yet received any job offers. I thought about going home, but I was quickly reminded that it would not be practical for me to go back to Sawyers because it was too far away from the developed areas. The unreliable communication and transportation systems made it almost impossible for a person to seek employment outside of the district unless he was planning on relocating. With such limited options, I needed to devise a plan rather quickly.

Receiving Our Marching Orders

After approximately two weeks of just camping out at the academy, a number of the trainees decided not to follow the rules anymore. They began getting up late and not doing their assigned chores. In other words, they were treating the facility as if it were an all-inclusive resort and not an academic institution. With that said, Ms. Stimpson decided to give us our marching orders. She came by the dormitory one morning and told us that we needed to leave because we had received our training and it was time for us to move on and make way for the next batch of trainees. Who would have thought that boarding school would be so accommodating that, even after graduation, the trainees would find it hard to leave? Whether we were ready to fly or not, we found ourselves being booted from our cozy nests by the mother bird.

Once again, what was about to transpire in my life was nothing that I can attribute to luck or coincidence,

Chapter 6

but to the overwhelming, undeserved grace of God. After receiving our marching orders, I was busy packing away my things, getting ready to go back home to the little farming district of Sawyers. However, my going-home plan was interrupted when a trainee came by and told me that Mrs. HoSang would like for me to contact her as soon as possible. The minute I contacted her, she said, "Desmond, did you find a job yet?" Before I could respond, she said, "If you are unable to find a job before you leave the academy, you can come and stay with me, because it is going to be very difficult for you if you go back to Sawyers."

She was absolutely right because, as I have stated, getting in and out of Sawyers had proven to be quite a daunting task, especially when you need to go job hunting. Moreover, Sawyers is a little farming district, and there is no meaningful employment in the area. With that said, I told her that I had not yet found a job and today was my last day at the academy because we had been asked to leave the premises. Without any hesitation, she said, "Get your things together, and I will come by and pick you up and you can stay by me until you find a job." Wow! What perfect timing! This outcome could be considered as having all the stars aligned in your favor. I went back to the dorm, completed my packing, and bid goodbye to my fellow trainees. In less than thirty minutes, Mrs. HoSang came by the academy. Before I went into the car, I looked around one last time because I could not believe that this was the end of my hotel management training. Now it all came down to everyone for himself. It was up to us to make the best of the training we had received. After my short trip down memory lane, Mrs. HoSang and I went home.

CHAPTER 7

LIFE WITH MY EXTENDED FAMILY

Upon arrival at her house, Mrs. HoSang took me to the little guest studio where I would be staying for the interim. The guest studio was quite unique and resembled a little castle. It was detached from the rest of the house, but a covered walkway connected it to the main building. It was round-shaped, equipped with a bathroom, and had a large king or queen size bed. Okay, I will not get too carried away with the labels, because the room was now being transformed into a man's castle.

Initially, I found it hard to believe that I was no longer a visitor but a member of the family. At no time was I treated any less than a family member. Neither was I forbidden from sitting around the dining table or on any of the couches and chairs. The warm welcome that was bestowed unto me by Mrs. HoSang and her family was genuine. It was not as if she were trying to make up for what had happened to me by my former foster parents because I did not mention any of that to her until twenty-four years later when I asked her for help finding a suitable home for my brother.

Chapter 7

In addition to always being welcome to sit at the table and enjoy meals with the family, Mrs. HoSang told me that I could help myself to a snack from the refrigerator or the pantry. With this royal treatment, I felt like I had booked into an inclusive guesthouse. After a couple of weeks, I invited Aunt Lucy to come and meet this wonderful person and her family.

Once I was fully settled in, it became a matter of finding a job. However, after approximately a month of searching, it appeared as though I needed a boost with my job search. I remember Mrs. HoSang came in one afternoon and asked me how the job search was going. I told her that I had sent out several applications but had not gotten any offers as yet. Immediately she responded, "Desmond, you leave it to me, I will make a few calls for you tomorrow." The following day, just around noon, she told me that she had arranged an interview for me with the Ambiance Hotel. Wow! How did she do it? What I had been unable to accomplish in almost a month, she was able to achieve in less than a day! Well, I should not have been surprised because she had plenty of connections. I should have outsourced my job hunting to her from the very beginning instead of following conventional wisdom. That goes to show you that having the right connections is just as important as the knowledge you need to do the job.

The next morning, I got up early and went to the Ambiance Hotel for my first job interview. The interview went well, and I was hired on the spot. I was assigned to the hotel engineering/maintenance department. After the interview, I ran home and provided Mrs. HoSang with the good news. She was quite happy for me.

Life with My Extended Family

Off to My First Fulltime Job

The following morning, bright and early, I commenced working for the Ambiance Hotel located at Runaway Bay, St. Ann. Upon arrival, my manager, Mr. Edward, welcomed me and asked me to accompany him to his office so that I could complete the necessary employment forms. After I was through, he went over the job requirements and the work schedule. Finally, he introduced me to my coworkers. In addition to being the manager of the engineering department, Mr. Edwards was also the food and beverage manager and the grounds and garden manager. This multidimensional manager was certainly a Jack of many trades.

The day was one to be remembered and, in the words of a Jamaican, it was all "cool runnings man!" This opportunity was beyond my wildest expectations. I was very fortunate to have been a graduate of a prestigious academy and to be awarded a full-time job with an all-inclusive resort. Once again, I found myself reminiscing on the very first day I had arrived at Aunt Lucy's with the hope that she would be able to provide me the very basics in exchange for whatever manual labor I could provide her. However, she did not view life that way. Instead, she helped me to accomplish the following: First, my basic education at the Sawyers All-Age School. Second, a two-year vocational and academic training at the Albert Town Secondary School. Third, a one-year hotel management training at the Runaway Bay HEART Academy. Finally, she allowed me to realize my first real job in the tourism sector. In times like these, I lament for my only brother knowing that he would have been a proud and resourceful

Chapter 7

member of society had he not being deprived of his future by the very foster parents who had been entrusted to care for him.

Although I was quite pampered by the HoSangs, I knew that it was time for me to find a place of my own. However, I was simply not making enough money to afford any of the in-town rental properties. Not being able to find an affordable place in the town meant that I would have no other choice but to move much further away from my workplace. However, just when I started to worry, the Lord intervened and provided me with yet another breakthrough. This breakthrough came to fruition one evening when I came home from work, and Mrs. HoSang said to me, "Desmond, my friends Mr. and Mrs. Christie live much closer to the Ambiance Hotel, and they are willing to rent you a room for a very reasonable amount."

Living with Mrs. HoSang and her family was a privilege and a wonderful experience that I will always remember and one that I will cherish for the rest of my life. It was a blessing and an honor for Mrs. HoSang to have invited me into her home and her life. Her children and her husband welcomed me into their lives with open arms. They never, on any occasion, treated me any less than a family member, for which I am more than grateful. Mrs. HoSang and I shared what I would describe as a wonderful mother-and-son relationship. We even shared a few jokes at times. Even though she had heard most of mine before, nonetheless, she would give me one of those "okay . . ." responses, followed by a big smile. She certainly had a wonderful sense of humor too. I must emphasize that when compared to the relationship I had with my former foster parents, this was a night-and-day experience. I would also like to

Life with My Extended Family

stress that Mrs. HoSang was not just another person, she was more like a mother to me.

On the one hand, I was very happy knowing that Mrs. HoSang would finally get back her guest quarters. On the other hand, I knew how much I would miss the wonderful life I had with my newly found family. It was one of those sad but joyful life experiences that reminds me to embrace change with a sense of optimism. After living with Mrs. HoSang and her family for approximately five months, it was time for me to pack my few belongings, head out to my new home, and commence writing the next chapter of my life's journey.

CHAPTER 8

MY FIRST ENDEAVOR

After a short ride, Mrs. HoSang and I arrived at the Christies' residence and Mrs. HoSang introduced me to Mr. and Mrs. Christie. After a brief discussion with the Christies, she reminded me that I was always welcome to visit her at any time. She then waved goodbye and affirmed that I was in good hands and that everything would be all right.

After Mrs. HoSang left, Mrs. Christie took me to my room so that I could put away my belongings. I could sense that the Christies were very excited to have me in their home and they provided me with a tour. Their bedroom was the only place that was off-limits, and I pretty much shared the rest of the house with them. Based on Mrs. HoSang's recommendation, they treated me like a family member rather than a tenant. I was very fortunate because on many occasions they would invite me to join them for dinner. I would like to emphasize that, although I was a tenant, Mr. and Mrs. Christie allowed me to sit and enjoy a meal with them at the dining table. In addition to the hospitable treatment, Mrs. Christie would clean my room whenever she was doing one of her "all-inclusive" cleanings. I was very happy to be living with this wonderful

Chapter 8

family. Sometimes I had to ask myself if I was really a tenant or a family member.

Seeing that the Christies had been more to me than just landlords, I would like to share with you a little more about them. First, they were classified as returned residents. This phrase is assigned to Jamaicans who migrated to England, United States, Canada, or another country in their early years, worked there for many years, sometimes to the age of retirement, and then returned home to Jamaica. This was true for the Christies. There was one issue, and it had to do with Mrs. Christie's health. She had a mental problem that affected her occasionally. To my knowledge, it never got to the point that anyone's life was negatively affected or was in any danger. However, on rare occasions, she would talk to herself all day long. Despite her illness, she was a very kind and loving person.

Hurricane Gilbert (Wild Gilbert)

By this time, I was fully settled in with the Christies and my much-appreciated multitasking role with the Ambiance Hotel. Despite having a job, I was always thinking about my next move in life because I was eager to learn something new each day. While I was contemplating my future career advancement, little did I realize that I was about to be shaken (literally) by a strong wind that was huffing and puffing hundreds of miles away.
On September 11, 1988, while I was working at the Ambiance Hotel, I heard the news that there was a massive hurricane, Gilbert, coming directly toward Jamaica. Based on the latest forecasts, it was poised to sweep directly across the island, from east to west, with projected wind gusts as

My First Endeavor

high as 145 miles per hour. I had never been through a hurricane before; therefore, I had no idea what to expect or how to interpret the effects of wind gusts. That day, my coworkers and I did not make any real preparations at the hotel or home. We simply did not believe that Gilbert was indeed a threat to the island and we disregarded all the warnings regarding the possibility of Hurricane Gilbert's making landfall on the island of Jamaica. Actually, I overheard a number of my coworkers welcoming (more like taunting) Gilbert. Although we had received many warnings and many pleas to prepare for the hurricane, we did not. We were hoping that the hurricane would take a different path away from the island.

The following day, I got up and went to work, because it was a typical workday and we had guests to cater for. I overheard people talking about the hurricane, but with no real sense of urgency. The tourists were inquiring about what preparations and evacuation measures we had in place. The only precaution we took was to relocate many of the guests from the second (top) floor to the first floor. As for everything else, our answers were simple and naïve. In fact, we would respond by saying, "No problem, man! Di hurricane nah come a Jamaica." ("No problem, the hurricane is not coming to Jamaica.") Well, we were in for a rude awakening because that morning we felt the wind gusts starting to pick up speed and intensity. Later that afternoon, we received several reports stating that Gilbert had finally made landfall at the eastern tip of the island and was causing major havoc to the island's infrastructure and natural environment. Sure enough, as the day wore on, the winds started rattling doors and windows at the hotel and the waves started eating away at the shoreline. I

Chapter 8

watched as the beachfront dissipated beneath the ebb and flow of the mighty waves.

Within a couple of hours, the hurricane was well on its way toward the western end of the island. The loss of electricity to the entire hotel was the first visible indication that this was undoubtedly going to be a very destructive hurricane. Well, no need to fear because we had a backup generator. Huge waves began crashing into the elegant, oceanfront dining room, while the little building that housed the standby generator was taking a beating. Shortly after that, I noticed that the roof had completely blown off the building that housed the generator. The situation was further complicated when a big wave crashed over the walls and flooded the entire building. Immediately after that, the generator failed and we lost power to the hotel. That was when it dawned on me that it was probably not a good idea for the hotel to have placed the standby generator housing directly on the beach. I was very fortunate that I had not been inside the building at the time the wave struck! After that close call, I made a mad dash to the maintenance building and joined my coworkers who were already hunkered down in a little concrete bunker.

As we were there hunkered down, we heard quite a lot of noise coming from the loose objects that were crashing into the walls and the roof of the building. I remember peeking out of the little window to see what the bangarang was going on outside. Not being able to see much from inside the bunker, a number of us decided to venture outside. Just before we reached the main lobby of the hotel, we found ourselves caught up in a powerful wind, and that was when we realized that Gilbert was really a monster. Or as we would say in Jamaica patois, "Raatid! Gilbert naa play." (Raatid is an expression of fright or surprise, while naa means not). Gilbert certainly reminded me of the big bad wolf. I mean, it was huffing and puffing and blowing down everything that happened to be in its path. With that said, we ran back into the bunker.

After the hurricane winds had subsided, we ventured out for a second time. It was an eerie feeling of calmness that I have never felt before. Not understanding the nature of a hurricane, we thought it had passed, so we started wandering around the property. We were all astonished, dismayed, and shocked by what we witnessed. The entire roof from one section of the hotel had peeled off and lay scattered about as if it had been hit by an explosive force. We were quite fortunate that we had taken the precautionary measure of relocating most of the guests from the top floor to the first floor. I also noticed that the elegant, beachfront dining room had fallen apart like matchsticks. The beachfront kitchen, along with its equipment and appliances, had been swept across the beach like seashells.

While we were out and about, a number of the guests came out of their rooms and warned us repeatedly that we were in the eye of the hurricane and the worst was yet to come, so we should get back inside immediately. I had never heard of a hurricane having an eye before, but I do recall hearing about the eye of the tiger. Okay, no need to try and figure this one out because it was apparent that we had no clue regarding the characteristics of a hurricane and we simply ignored the guests and continued to roam the property. However, we were interrupted when Mr. Edwards, the food and beverage director, engineer manager, grounds and garden manager . . . or should

Chapter 8

I just say, the multidimensional manager came running toward us.

He told us in stern words that the hurricane had not yet passed and we were now in the eye and needed to get back inside. At first, I thought he was kidding, or as Jamaicans would say, "A joke im a joke, man." Once again, we ignored all warnings and continued to display our carefree "no problem, man" attitude. However, minutes later, we heard a howling sound followed by a mighty gust of wind. That was when we realized that our multidimensional manager and the guests weren't joking. After that first encounter, we hurried back to the little bunker and remained there for the duration of the hurricane.

Once again, the hotel started taking a beating. At times, it appeared as though the second half of the hurricane was a thousand times more ferocious than the first. The hurricane came with a vengeance, as if it were saying, "Unnu retch unnu, unnu tink mi did dun." ("You little wretches, I am not through with you yet.") The hotel was being pounded from all sides. I remember when the wind finally subsided, none of us wanted to venture out as we had done after the first half. I guess we were not sure if it was all over or if the hurricane was simply playing tricks with our minds. For all we knew, Hurricane Gilbert was a three-eyed monster. As for me, I was not going to leave the bunker unless I was given the all-clear sign. After it was all over, the multidimensional manager came by the bunker and told us that it was okay for us to come on out.

Our first order of business was to make sure that all the guests were okay and accounted for. In some instances, there were as many as six guests to a single room due to the extent of the damage to the second floor. After we were through conducting a room-by-room inspection, we commenced the tedious task of removing the excess debris from the essential areas. Immediately after that, we were summoned to the kitchen to prepare the first "life after Gilbert" meal. The hotel had more than adequate propane and food, so we all rallied together and prepared the necessary hot meals. It did not matter what our titles were; that day, every worker who was present assumed a food and beverage role.

After all the guests had been fed, I decided it was time to go and see if Mr. and Mrs. Christie were okay and if the house was still standing. I did not know what to expect because the word-of-mouth news that was circulating painted a bleak picture of total devastation. We had also heard that many homes in the area had been destroyed beyond recognition.

The minute I stepped foot off the hotel premises, I was shocked by what I saw. The environment looked much different from the one I was accustomed to. The trees had lost most of their leaves and branches. I was able to see houses and other prominent landmarks that I had never known existed before. As I walked along the roadway, I witnessed downed power lines, blown-off roofs, tree branches, and just about any- and everything one could ever imagine. Even some sections of the road were covered with sand and stones that had been swept inland from the ocean. So much for my naïve, thinking that any label with the word mother (mother nature) included should automatically be kind, warm, and gentle. Thanks a lot, Gilbert, for debunking that notion. One thing I came to understand that day was the mere fact that, no matter how much superficial "superpower" titles we claim to have, humanity is surely

Chapter 8

no match for this world's uncontrollable forces. That day I was surely humbled and left in a state of awe after witnessing Mother Nature's destructive force.

Finally, I made it home. I was very surprised to see the Christies' house standing and, miraculously, having sustained only minor damage. The section of the house where my room was located had not sustained any damage either. We had running water but no electricity, so we had no other choice but to fire up the old "Home Sweet Home" kerosene oil lamps.

The next morning, I went back to the hotel and assisted with the preparation and serving of the meals for the guests. The hotel management training I had received from the academy allowed me to assume multiple roles. The guests didn't mind the inconvenience, but they were anxiously waiting for the roads to be cleared and the Donald Sangster International Airport to resume normal operation. Their stay had been transformed from being tourists to being survivors. Later that afternoon, the guests were transported either to the airport or to other hotels that had better accommodations. After the guests were all gone, the vacant hotel resembled an abandoned, broken-down shack. Surely this was one more reason to give God thanks, because after enduring a hurricane of such magnitude, things could have been a lot worse.

Next I visited Mrs. HoSang to see how she and the rest of the family were doing. Everyone was okay and trying to cope with the aftermath. At the end of the first week, all of the nonessential workers had been sent home. I was very fortunate to be one of the employees asked to stay on the job. We took on the roles of Jacks of all trades and assisted the management staff with the final shutdown operation of the hotel. Not like Gilbert had not done that for us already.

Opportunity Comes Knocking

After approximately two weeks of not doing much, I decided to start looking around for another job. Moreover, it was only a matter of time before all of us would find ourselves being laid off anyway. Once again, the answer to my prayers came shining through like a ray of light when I was contacted by a woman from the Runaway Bay HEART Academy. She informed me that Appliance Traders Limited (ATL) was seeking an air-conditioning technician trainee and that she would like to know if I was interested. Before she was through conveying the message, I provided her with a resounding "yes" to her inquiry. She told me that I should get in touch with the manager at the Appliance Traders' Ocho Rios branch as soon as possible. I was very excited because this would provide me with the opportunity to embark on a new and exciting frontier to learn about refrigeration and air conditioning with one of the most prominent appliance companies on the island.

The following day I went to Appliance Traders' branch in Ocho Rios, St. Ann, and finalized the hiring process. Although the compensation was less than my current salary, I did not let that deter me because I learned quite early that knowledge is far more rewarding than immediate financial gain. In life, there is always an opportunity cost to every decision, and this one came in the form of a

Chapter 8

salary reduction. Nonetheless, I tendered my resignation from the Ambiance Hotel, bid my remaining coworkers goodbye, and went on my merry way to commence yet another exciting career adventure.

CHAPTER 9

CAREER ADVANCEMENT

Appliance Traders was much further away, which meant that my job was no longer within walking distance. Not having a vehicle of my own (which is typical of most Jamaicans in the 1980s) meant that I had to rely on the public passenger vehicle service to get to and from work each day. Monday morning, bright and early, I boarded a minivan that commuted between Runaway Bay and Ocho Rios.[12]

There I was enjoying my cool ride into Ocho Rios, reminiscing on the days I had spent at the Ambiance Hotel and how Gilbert literally blew my job right out into the ocean. Regardless of how my job had ended, I was very excited about this opportunity and could not wait to get started. After a thirty-minute ride, the minivan finally arrived at the town square. I got off and walked approximately two blocks to the Appliance Traders building. The

---

12 If you have no knowledge of Ocho Rios, then all you need to know is the famous Dunn's River Falls. Dunn's River Falls are probably the most famous attraction for local and international visitors alike. Actually, the English translation for Ocho Rios is "eight rivers." Ocho Rios is located in the parish of St. Ann, which is also referred to as the Garden Parish because of its tropical beauty. There is a lot more to Ocho Rios, but Google Magic Wand will help you with your search.

Chapter 9

minute I arrived, I was greeted by the manager, Mr. Voss. He welcomed me and introduced me to the rest of the staff members, including the technical team. Shortly after that, he assigned me to work with one of the senior technicians, whom everyone addressed as Arby.

My Wishful Job Prospect

Just as I was settling down in my new role with Appliance Traders, another more interesting career opportunity sort of short-circuited my whole long-term prospect with the company. So, with that said, I will fast-forward to my final week at Appliance Traders Limited. One day while I was at work, Mrs. HoSang contacted me and told me that she had received a message from the Runaway Bay HEART Academy stating that I should come by the academy and retrieve a telegram that had been delivered addressed to me. Back in those days (long before cell phones) other than a direct landline phone (which very few people owned), a telegram was the next best means of communication used to deliver urgent messages. Therefore, receiving a telegram signified a sense of urgency, because either good news or bad news was awaiting the recipient. That night I was unable to sleep due to the overwhelming anxiety that was permeating my mind. I was wondering if my foster mother or any of my biological family members had fallen ill, been admitted to the hospital, or passed away.

    The following morning, I went directly to the academy to inquire what this telegram was all about. After reading it carefully, I was very happy to know that it was good news! It was an invitation for me to report to the Donald Sangster International Airport to attend an interview with

Career Advancement

the Airports Authority of Jamaica. This invitation was in response to the very first résumé that I had written to satisfy one of my writing assignments while I was a trainee at the HEART Academy. On the one hand, I was very happy with my current job at Appliance Traders Limited. On the other hand, it was a yearning desire of mine to work in some capacity at the Donald Sangster International Airport.

With that said, I decided to move forward with the interview. The interview was scheduled for Monday of the following week, which meant I had more than enough time to prepare. However, due to the unpredictable nature of the public transportation system, I was not about to run the risk of traveling from Runaway Bay to Montego Bay on the day of the interview. Also, the possibility of an accident closing down the only main road between Runaway Bay and Montego Bay was highly probable. To negate all these possibilities, I decided that it would be a good idea to stay with my sister Inez in Montego Bay over the weekend. Her home was ideal, because she lived approximately a fifteen-minute drive from the airport.

Saturday morning I packed a little bag and hurried off to the town square, where I boarded a minivan. After a long and daredevil ride, I finally arrived at Montego Bay. My first stop was at my sister's restaurant and bar, approximately a mile from the town square. The minute she saw me walk through the door, I could see the big smile on her face. She beckoned to her customers, saying, "Unnu watch-yah, unnu cuh me breda." ("Look here, this is my brother.") Then she said, "Cum sidung. Yuh ungry?" ("Come and sit down. Are you hungry?") Before I could reply, she turned to the chef and said, "Fix one lunch fi mi bredda deh." ("Serve my brother a lunch.")

Chapter 9

While I was eating, she came over, sat beside me, and said, "A weh yuh a du inna bay now?" ("What brought you to Montego Bay?") She was even more excited when I told her that I was there to attend an interview with the Airports Authority at the Donald Sangster International Airport. She was so happy she almost asked the chef to fix me another jerk chicken. Not really, but from my point of view, that was how her excitement came across.

My good news became her talking point with her customers for the rest of the afternoon. In other words, she was "bigging me up." ("Big me up" is a common Jamaican phrase which means to speak highly of someone.) After chatting for a while, she gave me the keys to her house and told me to go home and rest. Her philosophy was that I would do better in the interview if I were well rested. Sister Inez realized that being contacted by the Airports Authority for an interview was a golden opportunity and one that should not be treated lightly. As for me, I could not wait to see the dawn of Monday morning. If I could have sped up time, then I certainly would. Unfortunately, I had no other choice but to wait patiently just like everyone else.

Off to My Long-anticipated Interview

The long-awaited Monday morning finally arrived! I showered and got dressed in my very best attire. I was too anxious to eat, so I drank a cup of tea and went by the roadway to catch a taxi. After waiting for approximately eight to ten minutes, I saw a taxi coming toward me with horns blaring. I waved my hand vigorously, and he pulled over. I went inside and "hailed up" (greeted) the driver and he replied likewise. Within ten minutes, we arrived at the town square. From there, I took another taxi to the airport, because each taxi operator had been assigned designated routes.

Upon arrival, I got out of the taxi but had no idea where I was going. I signaled to a man who was slightly ahead of me and asked, "Yow boss man, could you please direct me to the Airports Authority administration building?" He pointed to a stairway that was located at the far end of the terminal building and told me to take it to the second floor. I thanked him graciously and hurried off in the direction he had indicated. Upon arrival, the receptionist greeted me and inquired about the reason for my visit. I told her that I was there to attend an interview, as had been requested of me. She told me to have a seat and promised that she would notify me as soon as the interview process got underway. According to the schedule, I was approximately an hour and a half early. In fact, I was the very first candidate to arrive at the interview.

Later that morning, I saw the other prospective candidates (all guys) arriving for the interview. Wow! I appeared to be just a youth (Small Boy) when compared to the other candidates. I wasn't sure if having youth on my side was a good thing in this situation. Well, no need to worry because my foster mother had told me on several occasions that what God has ordained nothing or no one can change. With that in mind, I sat calmly and observed the morning ritual as it unfolded around me.

Before I continue, I would like to provide you with a little drama regarding one of the candidates, whom I would like to address as Mr. Bombastic from this point forward. While everyone was seated, Mr. Bombastic came barging through the door as if he had been out jogging

Chapter 9

and all of a sudden remembered that he had an interview to attend. Not only that, but instead of jogging home and putting on his best attire, he decided to just jog right on into the interview. I guess he was quite familiar with the Biblical phrase, "Render your heart and not your garments." Anyway, I thought the receptionist was going to send him on his way jogging, but to my surprise, she told him to have a seat. The minute he sat down, he started talking to one of the other candidates as if he were the one conducting the interview. And to compound the issue, his decibel was turned up a bit too loudly for everyone's ears, including the receptionist's. He informed the person who was sitting next to him how well he knew the air conditioning supervisor and that it was the air conditioning supervisor who had recommended him for the job. He must have thought that knowing a current employee was all he needed to seal the deal and that everything else was at his discretion.

After sitting there for a good while, the interview process got underway. I was not keeping track of the time, but I do believe it was approximately 10:00 a.m. when the receptionist announced the name of the first candidate. He got up and walked toward the offices that were located at the far end of the administration building. I was unable to see exactly which of the rooms the interview was being conducted.

Guess what! Even Mr. Bombastic was interviewed before me. Okay, what's up with that? After he was through with the interview, instead of leaving the office, he started talking in a rather loud manner to one of the other candidates who had not yet been interviewed. He was saying things like, "Dem question caah tess me. Dem question de easy man." ("The questions did not faze me. They were quite easy.") I could see the expression of dissatisfaction on the receptionist's face. I do believe he detected that she was not pleased, so he left the room and that was the last time we crossed paths.

Okay, enough of Mr. Bombastic because I have a hilarious drama of my own coming up shortly. As the morning progressed, so did the interview process. All of the other candidates had completed their interviews, and I was the very last applicant left sitting in the room. This interview was certainly not on a "first come, first served" basis because I had been the very first person to arrive at the interview but was the very last person to be interviewed. From a business perspective, this interview must have incorporated the "last in, first out" (LIFO) method. I hoped I would at least have the opportunity to make a *lasting* impression on the interviewers.

If you think Mr. Bombastic was too much drama for one day, then think again. After sitting there for several hours, the receptionist told me to proceed to the conference room. Instead of asking for directions, I decided just to navigate my way around. All morning I had been good at asking for directions, but decided not to do so at the most crucial juncture of the interview process. So off I went. I walked past the main receptionist then took a left turn where an administrative assistant was typing away "clickety, clickety" on her noisy typewriter. She was so busy typing she did not even notice that a "small boy" had just sneaked by her.

I opened the door that was directly in front of me and went into a very prestigious office where a man sat behind his elegant desk, talking away on the telephone. I closed

Chapter 9

the door, which prompted the man's attention, and he looked at me and sort of knitted his brow, as if he were not expecting me. He signaled to me to have a seat while he continued his conversation.

I am not sure how long I was sitting in the office because my mind was preoccupied with the model airplanes that were strung out across his elegant desk. I am not sure why I was so taken up with the model airplanes. Probably I was wondering why he had so many toys on his desk while there were children at the orphanage who did not have any. Okay, the orphanage assertion wasn't really what came to my mind at the time, but nevertheless, it sounds like a good thought to entertain. Anyway, as I sat there, a little voice popped into my head and said, "You need to leave because this is not where you should be." I was not entirely convinced, so I remained seated.

Let me give you a glimpse of what was taking place on the outside while I was seated like a little snugly teddy bear in the elegant office. After the interviewers waited for a while and did not see me enter the room, they became concerned because it should have taken no more than a minute or two for me to walk from the receptionist's desk to the conference room. The interviewers waited a while longer because they assumed that I might have gone to the restroom or just stepped out for a marijuana smoke break. (Okay, please ignore the marijuana smoke break comment because marijuana smoking would most certainly be the last thing on my mind that morning.) Anyway, not seeing me come through the door after a reasonable amount of time, they inquired of the receptionist if I had gone to the restroom, stepped outside for a minute, or had to leave due to an emergency. What was more puzzling was the fact that the receptionist insisted that I had gone directly to the conference room where the interview was being conducted.

Once again, I was sitting comfortably in the wrong office while all this drama was unfolding on the outside. Finally, the man finished his lengthy phone conversation. However, instead of getting on with the long-awaited interview, he looked directly at me and said, "May I help you?" To which I replied, "I am here for the interview..." Before I was through, he said, "Oh no! You are in the wrong office. You should be in the conference room at the end of the hall," while pointing in the said direction. I got up immediately, exited the office, and went to the conference room where I saw three people sitting down chatting among themselves.

The minute I introduced myself, the HR manager, Mrs. Fairweather, said, "Where were you? I know you were here because you were the first person here this morning." Then she turned to the other two individuals and said, "Yes man, I remember seeing him in the same blue shirt sitting down on the chair when I came in this morning." I told them that I had gone into the wrong office, which I described. I also told them that the gentleman in the office was on the phone, and I waited until he was through because I had not wanted to interrupt him. Based on the description I provided, they were able to let me know that I had been in the general manager's office. Instead of getting upset with me, they all had a good laugh. Maybe if I hadn't been so taken up with the affairs of Mr. Bombastic I would have known in which room the interview was being conducted. Lesson learned, always MYOB (mind your own business). Well, there went my perfect day; and it was all because of Mr. Bombastic.

Chapter 9

This episode was more than a drama because I found out later that for a person like me to be invited into the general manager's office, I would need to have an appointment, check in with the receptionist, and then speak with the general manager's personal assistant. Therefore, being a person of my insignificant stature, it would be an honor to be invited into the general manager's office. That day I caused a serious breach of security by wandering off into the forbidden office. I hope the interviewers realized that I had no intention of just walking, but instead, working my way to the top. By the way, that was the first and the last time I set foot inside the general manager's office or had any direct conversation with him.

After the mishap, the HR manager said, "Okay, now that we are here, let's get on with the interview." Throughout the question-and-answer section of the interview, one of the interviewers, Mr. Tyson, said, "I noticed on your résumé where you mentioned that you want to become a great inventor. Tell me what you have invented so far?" Instead of saying "nothing" or "nothing as of yet," I had to mention a control switch that I "sort of" re-engineered. That was not an invention! No sir! Not at all! Anyway, Mr. Tyson knew quite well but did not want to ruin my dream of becoming a great inventor, so he gave me a pass. Or, in other words, he merely let that one slide by his ears.

After they were through with the interview, Mr. Tyson said, "Are you currently working?" To which I replied, "Yes, I am currently working for Appliance Traders Limited." He then turned to the other interviewers and said, "He is also one of Sammy's men." He was referring to the Airports Authority air-conditioning (AC) supervisor. As soon as Mr. Tyson was through speaking, Sammy happened to pass by the conference room. The interviewers took the opportunity to update him on my current job status. Although I was not scheduled to be interviewed by him, he took the opportunity to ask me several questions about air conditioning systems, which I was able to answer.

The possibility of being selected became even more apparent when he asked me if I had any knowledge regarding water treatment. I told him yes, and he proceeded to ask me a number of water treatment-related questions. Although my knowledge was minuscule concerning the chemistry of this subject, I was able to provide him with a brief overview of the pH balance as per alkalinity and acidity. Despite my limited knowledge, I could read his facial expression and surmised that he was very pleased with my response. Finally, he said, "If you are offered the job, would you be able to assist my team with upcoming projects?" With no hesitation, I gave him a resounding "Yes!"

Just as I was about to exit the room, the HR manager said to me, "According to the address on your CV, you are currently living at Runaway Bay and that would pose a problem if you were to accept this position because you are required to work shifts." I told her that I was in the process of relocating to West Green, which is approximately fifteen minutes away from the airport. I gave her my sister's telephone number and address for verification and future reference. I remember Sammy turned to me and said, "You seemed to do a lot of traveling. Which parish are you from?" To which a replied, "Westmoreland." Immediately, he turned to the electrical supervisor and said, "Sir T., he is one of your parish men too." I am not sure what difference that made, but at the time, anything to nudge me across the finish line was considered a value-added proposition.

Chapter 9

Finally, they concluded the interview and wished me all the best in my career endeavors.

The minute I walked out the door, I knew unequivocally that I had gotten the job. I mean, there was not even a shred of doubt in my mind from that moment forward. It was like getting a glimpse into the future. It was just a matter of when would I be contacted and how would I break the news to Appliance Traders Limited.

Before I bring this episode to a close, I would like to make one important point as it relates to my understanding of pH balance. While I was a trainee at the HEART Academy, I was fortunate to attend a one-week fire safety and water treatment course sponsored by the local fire department. Although this was considered optional, I was one of the first trainees to sign up. A number of the trainees stated that they did not see the need for this training, but I did not let that deter me because I realized that it might come in handy someday. And surely, this day was the day I found myself in need of such information. Therefore, my advice to everyone, especially the younger generation, is this: If the benefit (even though it might not be apparent at the moment) outweighs the cost, then I would strongly suggest that you do not neglect any knowledge that is made available to you.[13]

I also told Sister Inez that I had a strong feeling regarding the outcome of the interview and that she should listen out for a phone call or be on the lookout for a telegram from the Airports Authority. I also asked her if I could stay

---

13 Here is a little side note for you: I remember throughout the week-long course it took many tries before I was finally able to pronounce the word bromochlorodifluoromethane correctly. Go ahead and give it a try.

Career Advancement

with her until I found a suitable place to rent. Without any hesitation, she said, "Yes, man! Yuh know mi wi duh dat fi yuh man. Yuh a mi bredda, yuh know." ("Yes, you can! You know I would do that for you. You are my brother, remember.") My sister had gone out of her way to help several family members and total strangers without even considering the cost. I would not be the first, and most certainly would not be the last, family member she reached out to in such regard.

I was in no rush to leave Montego Bay because I wanted to spend as much time as possible with my sister. Moreover, I had not seen her in approximately two years, so it was a pleasure for me to spend the rest of the afternoon talking and indulging in a few laughs. She was also informing her customers that I would be working at the airport in the near future. My sister was even more optimistic than I was. Although I was highly optimistic, I had to remind myself on several occasions that the Airports Authority had not yet made me an offer so I should get back to Appliance Traders and take care of my bird-in-hand job. With that in mind, I bid my sister goodbye, boarded a minivan, and went back to Runaway Bay.

The Airports Authority's final decision came through much more quickly than I had anticipated. By Wednesday morning of that week, Mrs. HoSang contacted me and told me that I should get in touch with my sister right away. After work, I contacted Inez. She said, "Desmond, yuh get di jab at de airport, an dem want you fi start Monday so yuh fi cum down dis weeken, yuh hear." ("Desmond, you got the job, and the Airports Authority would like for you to start on Monday, so you need to come down this weekend.")

Chapter 9

This was the writing on the wall I had seen the minute I was through with the interview. Although the interview process appeared to have been nothing but smooth sailing, I found out later that my assumption had been wrong. Several years later, Mr. Tyson (my Airports Authority supervisor) told me that he had to plead with the HR Manager on my behalf because she thought that I was too young and that the job should be awarded to one of the older candidates.

The following day, I went to Appliance Traders, but my mind was preoccupied with trying to find the best possible way to break the news to my manager, Mr. Voss. However, the day was going by rather quickly, so I went into the breakroom, sat in a quiet area, and thought things over. After much contemplation, I decided to accept the Airports Authority's offer. First, working at the airport was a wish come true for me. And second, having the opportunity to be closer to my biological family meant a lot. With that in mind, I went ahead and tendered my resignation from the Appliance Traders Limited.

At the end of the workweek, I bid goodbye to my coworkers, took my belongings, and walked out of the building for the very last time. I certainly missed working for Appliance Traders because there had never been a dull moment at the company. I had acquired much practical experience and had been hoping to be promoted to the role of a senior project manager in the near future. However, it was now time for me to blaze the trail that led to the Donald Sangster International Airport. I had not yet informed Aunt Lucy because I wanted to be absolutely sure that I was indeed one of the chosen ones.

I spent the rest of the afternoon packing my belongings. Technically, I did not have much, so I was able to have all my things packed in less than thirty minutes. Then I visited Mrs. HoSang, and we talked for a while and reminisced about the time I had spent with the family. After we were through conversing, we bid each other goodbye, and I went back home and spent one last night with Mr. and Mrs. Christie, my landlords. Well, I should not refer to the Christies as landlords because they were more like my extended family.

I got up very early that Saturday morning, bid goodbye to Mr. and Mrs. Christie, then proceeded to the bus stop. After a short wait, a minivan came and was finally on my way to Montego Bay to commence the next chapter of my life.

CHAPTER 10

LIFE IN THE CITY OF MONTEGO BAY

My Wish Come True

While I was on my way to Montego Bay, I could not help but reflect on how the Lord had been really good to me. There I was, getting ready to embark on another new and exciting career opportunity. My primary objective was to take advantage of every opportunity that came my way. However, before I get too caught up with this job opportunity, I would like to reflect on my loving and compassionate foster mother, Aunt Lucy, who welcomed me into her home and into her life. Not only that, but her prediction in which she stated that, if I work hard in school, I would someday be working at the airport certainly had become a reality. However, none of this would be possible had it not been for the outstanding training I had acquired from the Albert Town Secondary School and the Runaway Bay HEART Academy. Finally, I would like to acknowledge the wonderful and enjoyable time I spent with Mrs. HoSang and her family. These are the

Chapter 10

compassionate individuals and outstanding institutions that laid the foundation beneath my feet.

After a long ride and with much to think about, I finally made it safely to the city of Montego Bay, St. James. From there, I boarded a taxi and went to my sister's home. My niece and nephew were very excited to see me and welcomed me into their home with open arms.

The weekend went by rather quickly, and before I knew it, it was approximately 10:00 p.m. Sunday night. However, instead of getting a good night's sleep, I found myself reminiscing on an event that had taken place at the airport approximately four years ago. Seeing that this was a fulfillment of prophecy and one that resonates in my mind to this very day, I would like to share it with you as well.

I remember my very first visit to the Donald Sangster International airport, which constituted my first trip to an airport. That evening I went with Aunt Lucy and Leighton to pick up her niece, Carmen (Aunt Carmen) and her daughter. We were a bit early, so we went to the waving gallery to see the arrivals and departures. The waving gallery (which does not exist anymore) was a designated area for families and friends who wished to bid goodbye or to welcome the arrival of family members and friends. People also used the gallery to relax while they watched incoming and outgoing flights. Although the sun was long gone beyond the horizon, we could still see everything due to the hundreds of lights that were scattered across the airfield. However, the most important aspect, at least for me, was being able to witness the landings and takeoffs of the aircraft.

Within an hour of entering the waving gallery, I saw a bright light coming from the western end of the island.

Life in the City of Montego Bay

As it got closer, I saw that it was a giant aircraft (British Airways). As it approached the runway, I was amazed by its sheer magnitude. It was the largest aircraft I had ever seen. However, the size was not what caused me to ponder; it was the fact that an aircraft of that size was able to glide through the air effortlessly like a bird. While I was there contemplating, the aircraft landed and taxied to the gate. As soon as the passengers started disembarking, we left the waving gallery and went to the arrival area to greet Aunt Carmen and her daughter.

Seeing that they had not yet cleared immigration and custom, I decided that I would go back to witness the takeoff of the giant aircraft. I was quite curious to see if a machine of such magnitude could really defy gravity. I sneaked away from the family and went back to the waving gallery. I watched anxiously while the passengers boarded the aircraft and the steps rolled away. Shortly after that, the aircraft was pushed away from the gate. I kept my eyes focused on the mighty aircraft as it taxied slowly westbound on the tarmac and then onto the runway. It then turned east and lined up with the runway. And behold, I watched as the "chariot without horses" took off down the runway with a mighty roar. Just before I could gather my thoughts, it lifted off the ground and, within approximately two minutes, vanished out of sight. It caused me to wonder if this was one of the objects prophesied by John in the book of Revelation. Most likely not, but this was my first trip to an airport and I was overwhelmed by the experience.

After the great revelation was over, I hurried downstairs and ran to the arrival area. However, I had another revelation awaiting me because, by this time, Aunt Lucy

Chapter 10

and the rest of the family were all worried, not knowing what had become of me. Everyone had cleared immigration and customs and was long gone, except for our party. As soon as I got close enough, the expressions on their faces were quite telling. They were not happy with me at all. Aunt Carmen and Joy had just gone through some fifteen hours of the hustle and bustle and were in no mood to go through another minute of delay. Aunt Lucy was very upset to the point that she could not help but take a swing at me with her handbag. Luckily for me, I was very light on my feet. I made a couple of quick steps backward and then slid to my right long before she could reload. Now you know that I was the one who pioneered the Cha-Cha Slide.

On our way home, I remember saying to Aunt Lucy, "Aunt Lucy, someday I would like to work at the airport." Despite the panic I had caused, she looked directly at me and, calmly and encouragingly, she said, "Listen to me man, anything is possible. If you go to school and study your book, someday you will find yourself working right here at this airport." Four years later, what had been merely wishful thinking had become a reality. Not only did I get to work at the airport, but I also had the opportunity to sit in the cockpit of the British Airways aircraft and help to maneuver it from one of the taxiways to the main terminal. I know this might sound a bit far-fetched so I will provide the detail of this inconceivable experience.

One Saturday night, while one of the British Airways aircraft was speeding down the runway, it sucked a bird into one of the engines and, as a result, the plane was grounded on the tarmac. The following morning while my coworker, Freddy, and I were working on the airfield, we drove over to where the aircraft was, and after a short conversation with the engineer, he invited us on board. I am not exactly sure what I said to him but what I do remember is that he invited me into the cockpit and, with his guidance, allowed me to start up the plane engines and help him navigated it from the taxiway back to the main terminal. I am quite sure that this was a violation of FAA rules, but I am not worried because I know you can keep a secret. This is an experience I will never forget! Not only did my wish of working at the airport come true, but my fantasy as it related to this mighty aircraft exceeded my wildest imagination.

Just to think about this experience of working at the airport made me realize that, once again, nothing is impossible with God! So, as the old saying goes, "Be careful what you wish for, you might just get it." This episode reminds me that words do have significant consequences and should not be used lightly. Luckily for me, I had wished for the attainable.

Let's get back to the night before my first big workday. After much tossing, turning, and reminiscing, I finally managed to get a nap in the wee hours of the morning. And before I knew it, my sleep was cut short by the crowing of roosters and the constant cooing of pigeons that were radiating through the house like a broken record. Not being able to sleep, I decided to get going even though it was quite early, approximately 6:00 a.m.

I got up, showered, dressed, ate breakfast, and hurried to the roadway to catch a taxi. Within a couple of minutes, I saw a taxi coming in my direction. I signaled to the driver, and he pulled over. I went in quickly and greeted the driver with a jubilant, "Yes mi brethren." He replied

Chapter 10

likewise and drove off. After approximately fifteen minutes, we made it safely to the town square. I got out and hurried off to the airport taxi depot, and from there took another taxi to the airport.

Upon arrival, I went directly to the administration building where I met the other two electricians, Deon and Trevor (but certainly not Mr. Bombastic), who had been selected from the thirteen candidates. After completing the necessary paperwork, we were greeted by our supervisor, Mr. Tyson. We accompanied him to the main electrical substation, where the electricians were stationed. Upon arrival, he introduced us to the other electricians who were on duty. After our meet-and-greet session, Mr. Tyson assigned us to work with the senior electricians who were on duty. I was assigned to work with Leonard on an electrical installation project. For the remainder of the week, I had the opportunity to work with the senior electricians on several installation and maintenance projects throughout the airport.

The overall scope of an electrician's job was to carry out the necessary installation and maintenance of the electrical systems throughout the airport. In addition to my electrician duty, I also assisted the air conditioning team (mostly nights and weekends) with their routine maintenance projects.

After collecting my first week's pay, I visited Aunt Lucy and surprised her with the wonderful news. The joy that was radiating from deep within her soul was all the words I needed to hear. She also reminded me of the comforting words she had instilled in me some four years earlier. She reinforced the point by letting me know that with God, all things are possible.

Now that I was working at the airport, I could not wait for Mr. Tyson to assign me to a project that involved working directly on the airfield. Working on the airfield was the most important and fascinating project I wanted to be involved with. Moreover, the configuration of the airfield lighting system and the landing and takeoff of the airplanes intrigued me greatly.

Finally, after a couple of months on the job, I was assigned to work with Freddy, a senior electrician, on a project that involved the taxiway, runway, approach, and obstruction lighting system. The airfield maintenance project would take anywhere from two to four weeks to complete, depending on the scope and nature of the issues encountered. On the first day of the project, I went to work extra early so that I would be ready and waiting. As soon as Freddy arrived, he and I packed the necessary supplies and tools into a vehicle and drove to the airfield.

The Donald Sangster International Airport has only one runway; therefore, we had to perform routine maintenance while the airplanes were landing and taking off. I should emphasize that there was no need for panic because the entire operation was fully coordinated between the electricians and the airport traffic controllers. For example, whenever the traffic controllers needed us to vacate the runway, they would use the two-way radio communication system and say, "Electrician, control tower." Then Freddy or I would reply, "Go ahead, control tower." Then the traffic controller would issue the command, "Please clear the runway immediately!" Freddy or I would acknowledge by saying, "Roger that, control tower." Finally, we would load all the tools into the vehicle, and exit the runway to a safe distance.

Chapter 10

I was very excited when I heard the controller give us our first clear-the-runway command. Upon hearing those words, I knew that I was about to witness the landing of an aircraft at close proximity. I had my eyes fixed westbound and watched as the aircraft approached the airport. My excitement and my adrenaline were at their highest when I witnessed the aircraft touch down on the runway. To my surprise, as the aircraft swooshed by, the exhaust from the engines was much hotter than anticipated. The odor of burnt fuel and burnt rubber emitting from the engines and tires was certainly not a breath of fresh air either. Regardless of the hot exhaust and the unpleasant odor, for the first couple of days, I was more taken up with this landing-and-taking-off phenomenon than completing the tasks I had been assigned.

At one point, Freddy said to me, "Tommy! Iah! Nuh worry yuh self, wi a guh out yah fi a long time. Yuh soon tap look pan di plane dem." (Tommy! Don't worry, we are going to be out here for a very long time. You will soon stop looking at the airplanes.") In other words, Freddy was letting me know that the landing and taking off the airplanes was a recurring event and that I would become bored of it really soon. Freddy knew exactly what he was saying because at the end of the first week, what had been considered a fun-filled job had morphed into an exhaustive, repetitive task. The heat, the stifling exhaust, the burnt rubber, and the screeching noise being emitted by the airplanes sucked the joy out of being on the airfield. At times, I would have done anything to be indoors or to find some shade to escape the constant heat. I hope the airline industry is demanding cleaner energy, because I have had enough of their dirty carbon footprints all over my lungs.

Life in the City of Montego Bay

Anyway, after working the day shift for several months, I was finally assigned to the three-shift schedule. On the 3:00 to 11:00 p.m. shift, Trevor, one of my coworkers, would cook some of the tastiest meals I had ever had. As soon as Trevor and I took control of the three-to-eleven shift, Trevor would assume responsibility for staffing the control desk. The desk was manned by one of the duty electricians whose sole responsibility was to coordinate the incoming and outgoing issues relating to the electrical systems throughout the airport. This person's role was more like a dispatcher.

At approximately 6:00 p.m., Trevor would start prepping the dinner. I did not know much regarding the art of cooking so I would pay close attention as Trevor went through the process of marinating the chicken with all the different seasonings. After he was through with the first phase of the cooking and the pot was simmering down, I would commence the most important task of the day by conducting a thorough visual inspection of the airport terminals, ramp, and airfield lighting systems. I would work at a timely pace because I knew that the meal would be ready within the hour. On my way back to the substation, I could smell the sweet aroma of the chicken from a distance. Well, that was not entirely true because nothing could overcome the burnt jet fuel and burnt rubber that was choking the air. As soon as I got back to the substation, I would complete the log and drop off a copy with the airport controllers.

With our most important task completed, we would sit down and enjoy our meals, which consisted of brown stewed or curried chicken with dumplings or rice. Come to think of it, I wonder why Trevor did not fire up the grill and jerk some chicken as well. Okay, that would be considered a little too much cooking on the job. Anyway, I would like to take this opportunity to say a big thank you to Trevor for teaching me the fine art of Jamaican food preparation, which I rely on to this very day. Today my family enjoys my cooking, but the credit really goes to Trevor, my former coworker and executive chef.

Academic Outlook

After approximately seven months on the job, my manager, Mr. Tyson, interrupted my work routine with a life-changing academic proposal. One day while I was staffing the control desk, Mr. Tyson approached me and asked, "Tommy, is everything all right?" To which I replied, "Yes, Sir. T." He then sat down on one of the chairs that were placed alongside the control desk, looked directly at me, and said, "Tommy, what plans do you have to further your education?" Instead of providing him with a direct answer, I hesitated for a moment; then I told him that I did not have any immediate plans. Although I was hoping to jump-start my academic career soon, for some unknown reason, I did not discuss that with him at the time. Mr. Tyson followed up by saying, "Tommy, look around, there are several workers in the electrical and other departments throughout the airport who started out working here as youths but have not been motivated or encouraged to further their educations. Therefore, they have many years of experience but not the education that would allow them to move up in the company, and I would not like to see you repeat their mistakes." Finally, he said, "I would like for you to take the opportunity of your youth and further your education."

Life in the City of Montego Bay

I simply could not believe what I was hearing. The real question for me was why a total stranger would be so concerned about another person's academic career. And most importantly, why me? Nonetheless, I assured him that I would like to further my academic career. Based on my response, Mr Tyson, said, "You can start out by taking a math course at the community college this coming September." He was referring to September 1989, which was four months away.

Shortly after that he got up, went to the blackboard that was located at the front of the room, and wrote an elementary algebraic expression to test my knowledge. However, what was shocking was the mere fact that I was unable to solve for the unknown (x). Oh boy! Here comes the dreaded flashback to the times when my brother and I had been physically abused and humiliated by our former foster mother because we were almost thirteen and eleven years old, respectively, and still unable to read or write. Not only that, but even to this very day, solving for the unknown has become one of the greatest mysteries. Well, that was not the important point I had in mind, so here is what I really want to say: Despite not being able to solve the problem, Mr. Tyson did not give up on me; neither did he laugh at me or ridicule me the way my former foster mother had. Instead, he looked at me and said, "Tommy, before you start community college, you and I need to spend some time and go over a few math topics." And that was where our conversation ended for that afternoon.

The following morning while I was at work, Mr. Tyson presented me with a copy of a math textbook and said, "Tommy, we need to schedule some time after work

Chapter 10

to go over the topics in this book." That very evening, Mr. Tyson and I spent approximately three hours working through many math problems. For the next four months, Mr. Tyson dedicated at least two hours of his time each day (this was necessary because of my snail-paced learning), Monday through Friday, prepping me for my first college course. At the end of the fourth month, he finally gave me the go-ahead to enroll at the community college. However, Mr. Tyson did not stop there, even while I was attending college, he would dedicate many hours of his limited time toward my academic career.

Jump Start My Academic Career

In September 1989, I commenced my academic career by enrolling in math and physics courses at the community college. However, I found out quite early that registering for two courses had been a bit too ambitious on my part. With that in mind, I postponed the physics course until the following school term. Despite taking only one course, there were times when my class schedule would conflict with my work schedule. However, Mr. Tyson would say to me in a calm voice, "Tommy, do not worry about the schedule; I will cover for you. All you need to worry about is your class." Surely, Mr. Tyson was a man of his word because whenever there was a conflict with my schedule, he would cover for me, spending anywhere from three to four hours per week covering my shift so that I could attend class. He also continued to tutor me even while I was enrolled at the community college.

At the end of the academic year, I sat the General Certificate of Education (GCE) exam. To my dismay, I was not successful on my first attempt. Nonetheless, Mr. Tyson did not get upset with me. I remember he said to me in a calm and comforting voice, "Tommy, I could have told you that you weren't quite ready for the GCE exam, but I wanted you to go and take the exam and use it as a learning tool for the upcoming term." He went on to reinforce his point by saying, "I am confident that you will do much better the next time around, so don't worry." Mr. Tyson was correct because I was able to identify my weaknesses and plan accordingly.

Genuine Personality Traits

Please bear with me while I take this opportunity to share a little with you regarding Mr. Tyson as a person and why he became a lot more to me than just my former supervisor. First, I do not want to give the impression that Mr. Tyson was helping me because he was aware of my childhood struggles. In fact, I only vaguely mentioned my circumstances to him some twenty years later, due to a situation concerning my brother. I want to reinforce the point that Mr. Tyson does not need to know about your past for him to care genuinely about your future, especially in the area of academic advancement. With that said, here are the facts without any bias or prejudice.

Over the past thirty-plus years since I came to know Mr. Tyson, he has dedicated his time, effort, and financial resources toward helping young people to achieve their academic dreams. I was very fortunate to be one of those individuals. Not only did Mr. Tyson spend many of his weekdays' tutoring, but he also gave up a lot of his weekends for many years tutoring children and adults

Chapter 10

(including many from his local district) without considering the costs.

On several occasions Mr. Tyson would review many math problems with me while we were traveling to and from different job sites (airports). While on our journeys, he would say to me, "Tommy, let us use this time to go over some math problems." Sure enough, we would use our travel time to review many math problems from a wide range of topics. There were times when I thought that this activity would impede his driving, but it did not. Mr. Tyson was able to concentrate on the road while tutoring me at the same time. Mr. Tyson is a true believer in time maximization.

Mr. Tyson told me that education became paramount for him when he stood at the doorway of his parent's home one morning and watched as his father went off to his all-day, labor-intensive job harvesting sugarcane for the local factory. He said that was when it dawned on him that he needed to do something to break the cycle so that he and his siblings could experience a better life. With that in mind, he decided that he was going to college, no matter the cost. The most important aspect of his conversation was when he told me that he had made a promise that he would do everything possible to make sure that his siblings gained access to education as well.

In another conversation, Mr. Tyson told me that he could have built a mansion for himself but didn't see how would that have benefited the rest of his family, especially his siblings, who needed financial support with their academic careers. Many people would have done the opposite, because it is a common tendency for us to use our talent and our financial wealth as the means by which we distinguish ourselves from each other, and at times, our own families. Unfortunately, this is also a subconscious, and sometimes subtle, practice and one that undermines the family structure. If we use our wealth and status to set ourselves apart from others, then our wealth and status become insignificant, and our life on this earth is of no real value.

I do understand that I have mentioned this before, but I believe it warrants a second telling. Mr. Tyson not only spent much of his time helping others academically, but he also spent a great deal of time and financial resources on his own academic advancement. To date, his academic accomplishments include a diploma in electrical engineering, a bachelor of electrical engineering, and a master of business administration (MBA). These accomplishments did not come easily for him. He had to overcome many challenges. One of the most noticeable obstacles was working in Montego Bay and attending classes in Kingston. This undertaking involved a six- to eight-hour round-trip commute. It was not uncommon for even the most skillful drivers to find themselves stuck in traffic or blowing a tire or two while navigating the treacherous potholes and tight corners that littered the road between Montego Bay and Kingston.

Mr. Tyson told me that one evening, after he was through working, he was quite exhausted and felt as though he was about to pass out. Despite his mental and physical fatigue, he pushed himself and made the treacherous journey from Montego Bay to Kingston to attend class. As soon as he walked into the building, his classmates told him that the class had been canceled. They continued by saying, "Mr. Tyson, we just don't know how you work all day and then drive for over four hours from Montego Bay

Chapter 10

to Kingston just to attend class." Mr. Tyson told me that he had replied in a jovial manner, saying, "A man's got to do what a man's got to do." Mr. Tyson went on to say that the joke was on him when he dozed off through one of his study sessions and his classmates turned to him and said, "Wake up, Tyson! Remember, a man's got to do what a man's got to do." Nonetheless, pursuing his academic career meant that he had to sacrifice a lot, such as money, sleep, vacations, and other tangibles and intangibles.

Mr. Tyson has been a mentor and a role model in my life. He has taken the initiative to care about the well-being of others even at his own expense. This is why I have dedicated this time to say a special thank you to Mr. Leroy Tyson for being such a wonderful mentor, advisor, role model, and friend to me. I could only imagine what Jamaica and the rest of the world would be like if we considered redirecting a little more of our drive, passion, and determination to help others succeed; not only academically but in all aspects of life.[14]

---

[14] The very same day I was reviewing this section of my autobiography, I received a phone call from Mr. Tyson. The minute I answered the phone he said, "Tommy, do you remember exactly what you said to me one day while I was tutoring you?" Sure enough, I remembered it quite well because the event that unfolded had left everyone who had been present laughing out loud for a good while. Here is the story in full: One day I became a bit frustrated because, after spending a tremendous amount of time studying, I still was unable to solve most of the math problems. Mr. Tyson intervened and, in a calm voice, asked, "Tommy, what seems to be the problem?" I replied, "Sir. T, it took three PhD people to write this book, so how could anyone expect me to solve their problems." Laughter erupted from everyone who was present.

No matter how insignificant this event may have seemed at the time, it is quite obvious that history has a way of repeating itself. And that was the case when Mr. Tyson told me that while he was tutoring two young men, one of them made the very same comment.

The Mysterious Reunification

After a couple of months of living and working in Montego Bay, I decided that it was time for me to go in search of my father and my brother. With that said, one bright and sunny Saturday morning, I asked my nephew (Mackey) to accompany me on a journey to conclude the final phase of my family reunification. That morning, we boarded a minivan that commuted between Montego Bay, St. James, and Savanna la Mar, Westmoreland.

Seeing that it had been fourteen years since I had seen or heard from my father, I was not sure how this trip would unfold. Besides, I had no idea if my father and or my brother were still at the house we had lived in throughout our childhood years. However, I realized that commencing my search at that location would be the best option. After completing the first leg of the journey, we got off at Line Gate, which is a little district in the parish of Westmoreland. From there, we took another minivan to Darliston, where I used to live with my father and my siblings. Darliston is a small district that is located in the parish of Westmoreland. I did not know exactly where I was going, but I had Mr. Manboard's house and woodwork shop (where my father used to work) as my most prominent landmark. With this information burned in my memory, all I had to do was to keep my eyes fixed on the right side of the street as the minivan swooshed around the corners, while driving on the left side of the road (in contrast to the United States). As soon as the vehicle was about to go by Mr. Manboard's property, I signaled to the driver with the usual "one stop, driva," he stopped the minivan, and Mackey and I got off.

Chapter 10

I immediately recognized the little trail that led to my father's home. Mackey, and we diverted off the main road onto the trail. As we followed the little trail up the mountain, I noticed several homes that I was quite familiar with. After walking for a while, I finally saw my father's little board house at the very end of the trail. In the words of Celine Dion, "It was all coming back to me now." My only concern was whether I would be lucky enough to find my father and or George at home. As my nephew and I continued along the dirt pathway, I looked to my right and noticed something that resembled a small animal curled up under an ackee tree. Not knowing what it was, we continued along the path toward the house. Shortly thereafter, I heard someone said, "Iah, Iah man." When I looked carefully, I noticed that the object that I had thought was an animal was a person.

Although I knew that it was not George, I was unable to tell if this person was my father. However, after seeing the person up close, I realized that it was, indeed, my father. I did not know what to do or what to say because I was stunned! I was left speechless! My father was unable to stand upright, which meant that he was unable to hug me or even to hold my hands. For some unknown reason, I did not run and embrace my father either.

I remember standing there in a daze. I was not only speechless because of my father's physical appearance, but more so because everything about me portrayed the Babylonian way of life my father denounced and despised passionately. That is, my head was shaved (not sporting any long nappy hair) and I had embraced the Christian faith (synagogue, as per my father), and adhering to the Babylonian doctrine. Not only that, but I was also attending school and eating forbidden food, such as meat and salt. Prior to this moment, I had no idea how much my whole being depicted the very essence of a lifestyle that my father had renounced. After having gone through a rapid mental process of elimination, I found out that my father and I had nothing in common that we could talk about.

Although my father and I were present physically, it felt as though we were absent mentally and emotionally. We were like two strangers from different worlds. Other than our DNA, it was quite obvious that my father and I had nothing else in common. The intangible characteristics of our lives were the reason why I was left speechless. In hindsight, I should have put more thought into how I would communicate with my father prior to my visit.

Nevertheless, my father reminded me of the abuse he had suffered at the hands of the "Babylonians" (police) who, he claimed, had "mashup" (badly beaten) his structure (body). I knew my father was speaking the truth, because I had witnessed firsthand this abuse and the horrific physical and psychological effect it had, not just on my father, but also on us, his children. I had overheard my father many nights moaning and groaning from chronic pain. After seeing my father's condition, I realized that, even after fourteen years, he still had not recovered from the physical abuse he had suffered at the hands of those rogue police officers. Whenever I think about this incident, it brings back painful memories of "the unforgettable day of injustice."

Due to the internal "noises" that were reverberating in my head, I am not sure if I did inquire of George. Moreover, my mind was going through one of those space-time continuum moments. After spending approximately one

Chapter 10

hour listening to my father, I had to say goodbye because I had limited time before the public transportation ceased operation for the day. Undoubtedly, it was a very sad day for me. It was certainly not how I had planned on celebrating the reunion with my father. It was very depressing knowing that I was leaving my father in such a deplorable state. But knowing how stubborn my father is, and how he deeply rooted in the Rastafarian doctrine, I refrained from offering any help or advice.

Based on my father's condition, I knew that if he did not receive immediate medical care, then it would only be a matter of time before he would succumb to his afflictions. I did outline his condition to Pauline and Paulette, but they told me that they had advised and even attempted to assist him in such regard, but to no avail. They also filled me in on one of their attempts that had not ended well for either party. After much persuading, my sisters were able to convince our father to at least go for a checkup at a Rastafarian doctor they knew. After his first visit, the doctor told my sisters that our father's diet needed a little salt and that they should try and persuade him in such regard.

Instead of trying to persuade him, my sisters made a special trip to his home and convinced him that they were there to spend the day and to take care of him (wash, cook, etc.). With their minds made up, my sisters set out to enact the real reason why they were there. That is, to add salt to his diet. They prepared his favorite meal and added a pinch of salt to it. They were hoping that he would not notice that salt was one of the "secret" ingredients. According to my sisters, the minute our father tasted the soup, he yelled out in a rather loud and painful manner, "Di I dem put harlot inna di I food an cramp di I jaw!" ("You guys put salt in my food and caused my jaw to cramp!") Finally, they told me that our father had become very angry and thrown away the food, along with the pot and the utensils that were used.

After visiting with my father, I tried very hard to get back to my daily routine, but I could not because I was deeply troubled by his physical and psychological state. Many times, I thought about visiting him so that we could sit down and have a meaningful conversation regarding his well-being and my understanding of life's "acceptable norms." However, it was quite difficult for me to put my thoughts into action because the last thing I wanted to do was to upset my father, thus causing further separation to our already nonexistent father-son relationship. Knowing how much my father hated Babylon and all its ways, how could I find it plausible to convince him otherwise? What could I say that would make my father deem our conversation acceptable? Would it be okay to indulge in a conversation about things such as my faith, my foster mother, my academic achievements, and my career aspirations? It is quite clear that what should have been a normal father-son conversation had become mental anguish for me. Therefore, other than our biological bond, my father and I had become two strangers drifting further apart with each passing day.

The one hour I had spent with my father was the last time that I had an opportunity to see or hear from him because he passed away shortly after that. I never had an opportunity to fulfill the father-son relationship I was hoping to establish with my father. Nor did I have the opportunity to inquire of him what was it about this

Chapter 10

world (or Babylon, as he portrayed it) that he despised so vehemently? Why did he feel the need to isolate us, his children, from the "norms" and cultures of this world? As I reflect on my father's life, I realize that the many unanswered questions regarding his life and his beliefs will forever remain a mystery. Most likely, my father could have lived a much longer life if the rogue police officers had not physically abused him. My father also complicated his illness because he chose to weave himself into many layers of impenetrable ideologies. Regardless of the situation, my father lived out his last days in a sad, lonely, and depressed state. My father passed away not having any of his children by his side to comfort him. Even to this very day, I am deeply saddened by this experience.

Opportunity Comes Knocking

Work at the airport went on, and I was now in my third year on the job. I was also pressing on with my 1990–1991 school term at the Montego Bay Community College. The GCE end-of-year math exam was coming up, and I was getting ready to spend many sleepless nights studying. In addition to my job and current academic progress, there was also another golden opportunity brewing on the horizon. It all started one day when I received a significant, life-changing phone call from Ms. Jasmin Wynter, the current manager of the HEART Academy. "I have been trying to get in touch with you for several weeks," she said. Then she continued by saying, "You have been awarded a two-year scholarship to study hotel management at the College of DuPage in America." After she was through speaking, I was left speechless. As I stood there with the telephone tightly gripped to my ears, I was unable to reply or even to whisper a single word. After a long pause, Ms. Wynter asked, "Are you there?" Finally, I was able to catch my breath. I do not remember what my exact response was. However, I do remember telling her that I was very happy to have been awarded this amazing opportunity. Not really in such an elegant manner but close enough. Anyway, I let her know that I had always envisioned myself going to the United States to further my studies.

So what was this scholarship about? This was an exchange program between the College of Dupage (COD) in Illinois, USA, and the Runaway Bay HEART Academy (RBHA) of Jamaica. This arrangement allowed four past students of the RBHA to pursue a two-year associate degree at (COD) in exchange for two students from COD to pursue an eight-month Hotel Management intern program at RBHA. After conversing with her at length, I came to realize that in order for this opportunity to become a reality, I would have to overcome several hurdles. The first came in the form of sponsorship. Ms. Wynter told me that I would need to secure sponsorship from a family member living in the United States. That is, a family member would have to provide me with the necessary financial affidavit of support. (I found out later that anyone could provide the affidavit of support not necessarily a family member). Nonetheless, this requirement is the financial proof needed by international students before obtaining student visas. This did complicate the matter, because I did not know of any relative living in the United States whom I could reach out to for any financial help. However, I went ahead and told her that

Chapter 10

I would make a few phone calls. I had no clue where and to whom I would direct those phone calls. Actually, I was merely buying myself time.

Ms. Wynter ended the conversation by reminding me to have the financial affidavit requirement completed as soon as possible. I was left with the daunting task of finding a family member who was currently living in the United States and who would be able to provide me with this affidavit of support. Aha! After many hours of searching through my memory archives, I finally remembered Aunt Lucy's sister-in-law, who resided in New York. Without any hesitation, I went ahead and contacted her. However, she was unable to provide me with the affidavit of support. Once again, I went back to the drawing board to see if there were any alternatives, but I had exhausted all my options. Well, it was more like my one and only option. I was very disappointed knowing that I would not be able to take advantage of this once-in-a-lifetime opportunity.

Later that week, I contacted Ms. Wynter and told her that I did not have any family members living in the United States to provide me with an affidavit of support. I suggested that she go ahead and award the scholarship to another trainee. I was quite surprised when she said, "Desmond, I do not know you personally, however, based on the testimonies that I have heard concerning you, there is no way I am going to give up on you. I am going to work with you to the very end. I will not give this opportunity to anyone else because you have earned it." She went on to say, "It took me several weeks just to get in touch with you, therefore, we do not have much time, but I am going to exhaust all of the available options." I am not sure what else we discussed, however, after she hung up, I was left

Life in the City of Montego Bay

holding the phone at my ear for a while, not realizing that our conversation had ended. I was left speechless regarding what Ms. Wynter had said.

I did not have much to contribute to the conversation, so all I had to do was to wait for Ms. Wynter's follow-up phone call. The next day she contacted me and initiated a brainstorming conversation. We went over several options, but nothing seemed to stick. She said, "Desmond, seeing that you are working for the airport is it possible for you to contact the manager of the airport and ask him for some financial assistance?"

Having no prior knowledge of the Airports Authority's internal structure, one would conclude that Ms. Wynter's proposal was quite reasonable. However, seeing that I was quite low on the totem pole, I came right out and told her that it was highly unlikely that the airport would do anything for me in this regard. Not only that, but Mrs. Wynter was asking me to contact the manager, who was the head of the entire operation of the Donald Sangster International Airport! However, not wanting to give Mrs. Wynter the impression that I had given up without trying, I let her know that I would pursue that option. She ended the conversation by saying, "Desmond, please get in touch with me by tomorrow and let me know the outcome." Come to think of it, wouldn't this have been a good time for me to just walk right into the general manager's office as I had on the day of the interview.

Nevertheless, seeing that I had not yet made a formal request for any assistance, it would have been foolish of me to give up just because I perceived that the odds were not in my favor. With that said, the following day, I spoke with Mr. Tyson and informed him of the scholarship that I had

Chapter 10

been awarded. I let him know that for me to proceed, I needed to provide proof of financial support. I also inquired of him if the Airports Authority would provide me with any financial assistance in such regard. Mr. Tyson told me that he was not sure what the Airports Authority would do in this situation, but that he would do everything to convince the manager that this would be for a noble cause.

The following day Ms. Wynter contacted me via the phone and asked if I had spoken to the manager regarding the affidavit. I told her that I had not yet spoken with the manager directly; however, I had spoken with my supervisor, and he assured me that he would do everything possible to get the message across. "Due to the urgent nature of this situation, there is just not enough time!" she said. "We need to come up with a plan today! Give me the name and phone number of the general manager, and I will contact him on your behalf." I did accordingly; then she said goodbye and hung up the phone. Approximately two hours later, she contacted me and told me that she contacted the manager and explained the situation to him and he assured her that he would review her request and get back with her as soon as possible. However, I did not hear an upbeat mood in her voice, which led me to believe that she was not too optimistic that the manager would follow through on his promise.

Another couple of days went by with no follow-up call from Ms. Wynter. However, around the fourth day, she contacted me to find out if I had heard anything from the airport manager. I told her that I had not. She sounded a bit frustrated and said, "Do you realize that I have contacted him several times since we spoke, and he kept on giving me the runaround." I did not know what to say because if she was experiencing difficulty convincing him to act, then we might as well give up because it would be almost impossible for me to do anything to influence the outcome. It was evident that I would not stand a chance.

After several unsuccessful attempts, Ms. Wynter contacted me and said, "Desmond, we are getting nowhere with the manager, so we need to take another approach." We both went into the silent zone for a brief moment. As for me, I had absolutely nothing further to contribute to the conversation. In fact, I had long given up on this scholarship. So, while I was there waiting to hear the click/hang-up sound coming through the phone, Ms. Wynter said, "Desmond, who do you work for?" With not much enthusiasm, I told her that I currently work for the Airports Authority. Immediately, she followed up by saying, "Desmond, do you realize that the Airports Authority and the HEART Academies fall under the Human Resource Development of Jamaica!" I knew that to be true regarding the HEART Academies, but as for the Airports Authority, that I had not known.

Then she said, "Okay, I will go ahead and contact the Airports Authority in Kingston [capital of Jamaica] on your behalf." By this time, I was like a dead salmon floating downstream. In other words, I was just going with the flow. Not only that, but if our cause turned out to be futile at this level, then it would only complicate the matter of escalating our cause to the highest level of the organization in which I existed only as a number. Once again, I was leaning on my own understand and forgetting that with God, all things are possible. In any case, the situation was now squarely in Ms. Wynter's hands, and she seemed to have regained her sense of optimism. Even

Chapter 10

though I was unable to fulfill my requirements, that did not stop Ms. Wynter from working tirelessly on my behalf.

The Miraculous Breakthrough

Within two days, Ms. Wynter contacted me and, in an upbeat and joyful tone, she said, "Desmond, our hard work and perseverance have finally paid off. I contacted Mr. Trevor Waite, the vice president of human resource and development of the Airports Authority, and explained our situation to him, and he promised me that he would personally address our concern and we will hear from him shortly." She continued, "I also let him know that we are not getting any support from the general manager at the Sangster International Airport." Once again, I was left speechless because Ms. Wynter had taken my cause to the highest level in the organization and was now referring to a person whom I have never heard of or met before. All I could do was simply thank her many times over.

The next day, September 6, 1991, to be exact, Ms. Wynter contacted me and told me that Mr. Waite had sent her a letter stating that the Airports Authority had provided me with two-year study leave and financial support in the sum of one year's salary. She also told me that Mr. Waite had sent me two copies of the contract, one to keep for my records and the other for me to sign and return to the HR manager at the Montego Bay division. While I was on the phone listening to what Ms. Wynter was saying, I kept checking to make sure I was awake and not dreaming.

Once again, I was left speechless! Surely this was not a dream, but a dream come true! And it was transpiring right before my eyes. This was yet another miracle to remind me that with God, all things are possible if I only believe. I can assure you that this was one of the happiest days of my life. I was so caught up in the moment that I even forgot that I was still on the phone. Not having much to say, my only response was to emphasize how happy I was and how much I appreciated her relentless perseverance. I just could not find enough words to thank her. Once again, she said, "Desmond, up to this point I have not met you in person but based on what I have heard from everyone at the academy, there is no way I was going to give up on you." Today, I can truly say that, even when the odds were overwhelming and the process seemed impossible, Ms. Wynter never quit. She held dearly to the premise, "Where there's a will, there's a way."

On September 9, 1991, I received two copies of the contract via the Airports Authority interoffice mail. As per the instructions, I signed and returned the designated copy to the HR manager. I also provided Mr. Tyson with a copy of the contract. Being a person who regards knowledge as paramount, words could not begin to explain how happy Mr. Tyson was when he found out that I was one step closer to pursuing my academic studies in the United States of America.

Meeting My Trusted Mediator

The next morning, bright and early, I went to the Runaway Bay HEART Academy to meet this wonderful person who had been working tirelessly on my behalf ever since our first phone conversation approximately three weeks before. Upon arrival, I was very excited to see Ms. Wynter.

Chapter 10

I was at a loss for words, but I managed to express my thanks and gratitude to her for the hard work, and most of all, the perseverance she had demonstrated on my behalf. Once again, her reply was, "Not a problem Desmond, you have earned this award." After a short discussion, she emphasized the need for me to go to the United States Embassy in Kingston and apply for a student visa. I thanked her again, said goodbye, and went to the bus stop to catch a minivan back to Montego Bay.

The Risky Endeavor

On my way to the bus stop, I reconsidered and decided that it would be a good idea for me to go to Kingston and stay overnight with Leighton so that I could increase my chances of being allowed into the US Embassy the following day. So, instead of boarding a minivan back to Montego Bay as I had originally planned, I boarded a minivan and went to Ocho Rios instead.

As soon as the minivan arrived at Ocho Rios, it started getting dark, which caused me to start second-guessing my decision. I had no experience finding my way around Kingston in the daylight hours, so can you imagine how difficult it would have been for me at night? Even the little voice inside my head kept reminding me of the clear and present danger I was about to face if I were to embark on such a risky undertaking. To further complicate the issue, I did not have Leighton's actual address or phone number, only a vague idea of where I was going. Even if I had a phone number, I would have had to search diligently for a payphone that worked because I was living in the BCP (before cell phone) era. To make matters worse, Leighton had no idea I was coming. Therefore, he could have been somewhere on the island of Madagascar, enjoying his vacation.

Nonetheless, I chose to press ahead and defy the overwhelming evidence and commonsense reasoning that this was indeed a risky undertaking. With that said, I boarded a minivan that commuted between Ocho Rios and Kingston. As I sat in the minivan, wrestling with the little commonsense voices in my head, I was continually being interrupted by the conductor who kept shouting, "Kingston ova yasso. Last trip fi di day." ("Kingston over here. This is the last trip for the day.") As soon as the minivan was filled with passengers, the conductor signaled to the driver, saying, "Driva! A yuh dis!" ("Driver it is your time!" or, "Time to go, driver!") The driver came into the minivan, cranked up the engine, and revved it several times. Then he circled one last time just to see if there was any last-minute passenger who needed a ride to Kingston. A last-minute passenger is a person that you would see a good distance off running toward the minivan with a whole heap of bangarang, shouting "Driva, driva, wol-awn de driva!" ("Driver, driver, please wait for me driver!") Most of the time, there would be no space left in the trunk of the vehicle and this person would resort to asking each and every passenger to hold one or two pieces of his or her bangarangs.

That night, we were lucky not to have such a person. The driver drove to the little petrol station and shouted to the attendant, "Full mi up de, boss." ("Fill up the tank, sir.") As soon as the attendant filled the tank and cleaned the windshield, the conductor shouted one more time, "Driva! A yuh dis!" Before we commenced our long journey to Kingston, the driver honked the minivan horn

Chapter 10

several times then maxed out the volume of his mobile jukebox. My, my, his jukebox was extremely loud! The base must have been maxed out because I could feel my internal organs vibrating.

Now there was no turning back, I was on my way to Kingston. Or at least that was what I thought. After going less than a quarter of a mile from the bus terminal, the minivan engine started sputtering. The minivan sounded as though it were experiencing a terrible case of the hiccups. Minutes later, two of the passengers sitting to my right shouted, "Driva, a wah de wratid a gwaan wid di bus?" (Driver, what the wratid [a crude Jamaican expression] is going on with the bus?") Several of the passengers bombarded the driver with their expert advice. They were saying things like, "Driva, put di van in a neutral an rev up di engine an bun aff di ile aff de spark plug." ("Driver, put the van in neutral and rev the engine to burn off the excess oil that accumulates on the spark plugs.") The driver did not answer or pay them any attention because he was too busy trying to keep the engine going. He then placed the minivan in neutral and revved the engine for a while. I guess when all else fails, why not follow the advice of a few inexperienced wannabe mechanics.

By this time, everyone started getting a bit frustrated. Despite the relentless efforts by the driver to keep the engine running, it finally died. And that was what it took to "spark" a mass confusion among the passengers. A number of the passengers were quite sympathetic to the driver's plight, while the others were giving him and the conductor an earful. You could hear them saying things like, "Driva, you fi tek de ole mashup bus aff di road!" ("Driver, you need to take this messed up bus off the road!") And in

Life in the City of Montego Bay

every bad situation, there is always a comical person in the mix. With that said, I heard a guy from behind me shouting, "Driva a way u nuh sell di bus an use di money buy an engine?" ("Driver, why don't you sell the minivan and take the proceeds and buy yourself an engine?")

I do believe that the driver had heard enough of the passengers' smart remarks because immediately after that he shouted, "Unnu shut up unnu mout in di bus!" ("You all need to be quiet inside the bus!") The driver tried several times to start the engine, but whatever happened, it really did a number on the engine because it never recovered; at least not while I was present. Who knows, it could have been the deafening jukebox that drained the life out of the engine; just a thought. Or could it be that I was the Jonah (Biblical reference) whom they needed to throw off the bus?

By this time, it was quite dark, and the convincing voice that had been talking to me from the moment I set out on this journey, spoke to me one more time: "Desmond, please get off this minivan and contact Mrs. HoSang, because you have no idea where you are going and the danger that lies ahead!" With no further hesitation, I got off the minivan, searched diligently for a working phone, and contacted Mrs. HoSang. I explained to her what had happened, and immediately she raised her voice at me and said, "Desmond! Why are you going to Kingston this time of the night for! It is dangerous for you because you do not know Kingston well enough to be traveling alone at night!" Then she said, "Come and stay over by me and you can leave early in the morning, because traveling around Kingston at night with no idea of where you are going is just not safe!"

Chapter 10

That was all it took to convince me that I was doing something really stupid. Moreover, this was exactly what the convincing voice inside my head had been telling me since the minute I had embarked on this risky journey. I guess I needed to hear it from an external voice for me to heed the warning. With that said, I boarded a minivan and went back to Runaway Bay. As soon as I got home, Mrs. HoSang gave me a delicious meal and reinforced her point regarding traveling to Kingston at night, especially when I did not know where I was going. After I was through eating, she told me to get some rest and that she would wake me in the morning.

The Daredevil Driva

I woke up very early the following morning, showered, dressed, ate breakfast, bid goodbye to Mrs. HoSang, and hurried off to the bus terminal. I boarded a minivan and went back to Ocho Rios, and from there took a taxi to Kingston. I am not sure why I ended up choosing a taxi and not a minivan. Probably it had everything to do with the dramatic experience I had with the minivan the previous day. Regardless of the reason, it turned out to be a very risky adventure. Actually, for the first couple of minutes, the ride turned out to be a lot more frightening and heart-pounding than I had anticipated. First, the driver was speeding as if he had been given a personal invitation by the devil and was on his way to hell. He was going around the corners as if he owned the road and there were absolutely no other vehicles coming from the opposite direction. One would think that after several close calls and a whole lot of whispered "Laud Jeezas!" (Lord Jesus!)

Life in the City of Montego Bay

by the passengers, the maniac driver would have gotten the point that he needed to slow down. However, he did just the opposite and decided to stretch his luck.

Just as we approached the plateau and started the steep descent down Mount Rosser, the driver went around a corner and came head-on with a wide-bodied dump truck. Mount Rosser is an area that is dreaded by most commuters because of the perceived toxic mud lake at the foot of the mountain. This mud lake is the residue from the Alcan Bauxite alumina treatment process. God was on our side that day because the driver had to leave the road entirely and park the car in a little gouged-out area left behind by the parish council roadwork crew. When the passengers, including me, saw how close we had come to death's door, in a frantic but unified voice, we gave the driver an earful. From that point forward, he heeded the warning and stopped driving like a damn lunatic. So, after a long and, yes, frustrating ride, I finally made it to Kingston. Back in those days, a taxi would carry anywhere from six to eight people including the driver. However, a typical minivan would carry anywhere from ten to fifteen passengers. Therefore, the taxi drivers would drive a lot faster to make more trips. Anyway, please remain seated with your seatbelts fastened because the next phase of my journey comes with even more turbulence.

Here comes the next drama: First, I did not have any idea regarding the Kingston minivan transportation system. In other words, I did not have a clue what bus commutes where. With that in mind, I asked one of the passengers for directions to the US Embassy. I remember the lady said to get off at the red and black gas station at the corner of Hope Road, and the embassy is right there.

Chapter 10

Within a couple of minutes, I saw a Toyota Coaster minivan coming at a high rate of speed. It came to a stop, and several passengers, including me, started pushing and shoving to get on board. As soon as the last passenger was on the step, the driver accelerated at full speed, as though he were being chased out of town by an angry mob. There were no empty seats on the bus, so I had to stand in the aisle and hold onto the overhead rails.

Although the bus was packed beyond the designated capacity, the driver continued to pick up passengers along the way. The bus was completely packed to the point that I was unable to move my feet. To complicate the matter, I was unable to see where I was going. Just when I thought the bus could not accommodate another person, the driver stopped to pick up even more passengers. After failing to get the passengers into the bus, the conductor started banging on the windows, shouting, "Yow! Yow! Move dung inna de bus!" ("Hello! Hello! Move down in the bus!") An elderly woman who was standing before me shouted at the conductor, "Conducta, yuh nuh si say de bus full?" ("Conductor, don't you see that the bus is full?") Instead of heeding her concern, the conductor replied comically, "Nuh tell mi wen bus full! Mi nuh wen bus full! Yuh si wen mi put one smadi inna di front an wan drap out a de back, den me nuh seh di bus full." (Lady, do not tell me when the bus is full! I know when the bus is full! The bus is full when I put a passenger in the front and another falls out the back, then and only then, I know that the bus is full.")

After approximately twenty minutes of the fast and furious, "ram-dem-in," motor vehicle experience, I finally got a glimpse of the red and black petrol station I had been told to look for. I rang the bell and, with much pushing and shoving, I managed to get off the bus. Wow! I was happy to be alive after such a chaotic ride!

The Joy and Disappointment Associated with the US Embassy Visa Process

I walked briskly to the embassy and joined the queue that already stretched a good distance down the street. This was my first time visiting the embassy, so I just followed the people ahead of me in the queue. Back then, the embassy did not issue appointments for first-time visitors. Therefore, we had to stand in long queues for many hours before the process commenced. In addition to the "first come, first served" method, the process was further complicated because many of the people who were in the queue weren't there for visas. They were there hoping that they could make a quick dollar by selling their places in the queue to someone who needed them. So much for "first come, first served." Although I was a good distance from the front of the queue, I had a very good chance of being allowed inside the embassy that day. Therefore, I did not have a need to purchase a closer place. If you were near or at the back of the queue, there was a strong probability that you would either have to purchase a closer place in the queue from one of the hustlers or come back to the embassy the following day.

After standing in the queue for a good two hours, the security guard opened the gate, and the process got underway. I was escorted into an open hall where approximately 150 people were waiting to present (more like to plea) their cases to the US representatives/diplomats. I will refer to them as diplomats from this point forward. I can assure you

Chapter 10

that the diplomats had their work cut out for them. While I was sitting in the open hall, I saw two women crying. I remember asking myself why these women were crying. Had they forgotten the words of Bob Marley, in which he clearly stated, "No woman nuh cry"? Being naïve about the process, I thought that if they did not get through today, they could just come back tomorrow or the following day and try again. Once again, this was my first time visiting the US Embassy, which meant that I had absolutely no knowledge regarding the process. Later that afternoon, I came to realize that many of those individuals were told not to come back for one, and in some cases, two years. I guess that is one way to keep people from showing up every day. And knowing Jamaicans, we would join the queue many times in one day hoping to present our cases to different diplomats.

After a long wait, I was escorted into yet another open hall located on the second floor. I sat there and observed as people were signaled one after the other to approach the diplomats who were located in booths. After twenty-five to thirty minutes, it was finally my turn to face the diplomat. I stepped up to the booth and presented the man behind the counter with all my documents. He flipped through the stack of papers twice then asked, "Where is your I-20?" I did not have a clue what document he was asking for or what an I-20 was.

The only thing that flashed across my mind was how my father had taught me to place the letter 'I' at the beginning of every sentence and as a substitute for many words such as me, my, and you. With that vivid flashback, I thought I was being interviewed by a Rastafarian. Probably I should have replied, "Yow Rastaman, I an I nuh have no I-20 seen!" Okay, I am getting carried away so let me get back to the process at hand. Instead of providing him with an answer, I chose to repeat his question, "I-20?" He replied, "Yes, I-20, the international student immigration document that you should have received from the college." I remained silent because I had no clue. Not wanting to be viewed as clueless, I went into stutter mode "Aaa . . . aa," followed by a long pause. Not knowing what to say, I finally told him that I had no idea what document he was inquiring about. He then told me that he was unable to continue the process without the I-20 form. His exact words were, "The I-20 is the most important document you should have received from the college." After seeing the disappointment all over my face, he reinforced the point by saying, "Even if I go ahead and award you the visa, without the I-20, you could be denied entry at the port." He advised me to contact the college, obtain a copy of the I-20 form, fill it out, and come back to the embassy.

I remember walking away, feeling very sad. But I was certainly not going to cry like the women I had witnessed earlier that afternoon. While I was walking by the waiting area, a woman came up to me and said, "Bwoy, mi nuh how yuh feel, but hush yuh wi get true nex time." ("Boy, I know what you are going through, but you will get through the next time.") I guess this woman had suffered several rejections and was speaking from personal experience. I did not know her, but she certainly gave me a boost of confidence.

That afternoon I met the other three trainees who had also been awarded scholarships. Their bids for visas were also denied for the same reason. We contacted Ms. Wynter and broke the bad news to her. She immediately

Chapter 10

contacted the College of DuPage and had the I-20 forms expressed to her.

Shortly after that, Ms. Wynter contacted me to make sure I had everything in place and was "fired up and ready to go."[15] Ms. Wynter followed up by asking, "Desmond, do you have your spending money?" Instead of providing her with a resounding, "Yes, I do," I stuttered over a couple of words before I finally had to say, "No." I let her know that the airport had not yet provided me with the check (or cheque if you are a member of the British Commonwealth) for the one-year paid study leave as promised. As for me, I was really fired up, but not having any money meant that I was not yet ready to go.

I was now facing yet another dilemma and was in need of another miracle. If you think that my unfortunate situations were causing Ms. Wynter to experience heartburn, then to that I say, think again. Just by letting her know, at the last minute, that I did not have any money must have given her the worst stomach ulcer. She raised her voice and said, "What do you mean you do not have any spending money?" This time, I kept really quiet. She continued, "Are you telling me that you have been working for almost three years and you have not saved anything?" I told her that I had just used up my entire savings to purchase a car and, unfortunately, it had been destroyed by fire. Well, there goes the only thing that was fired up. After I was through explaining my misfortune, she lowered her voice and said, "Desmond, don't worry. I am going to try and see what I can do for you."

---

15 Let me give credit to President Obama for the "fired up, ready to go" phrase. Well, the credit should really go to the originator, Ms. Edith S. Childs.

I felt embarrassed because the more Ms. Wynter did for me, the more I needed her help.

When it was all said and done, once again, Ms. Wynter came through like a never-ending supernova. She contacted the owner and operator of the Franklyn D. Resort in Jamaica, Mr. Frank Rance, on my behalf, and I became the beneficiary of a check for $875 US. Before I proceed, I would like to take a minute to express my sincere thanks and gratitude to Mr. Rance for his overwhelming act of kindness in this regard. His generous support made it possible for me to finance my first month's rent, food, and other college-related expenses. I indeed owe him a debt of gratitude. Please see Appendix B for details regarding my first face-to-face visit with Mr. Rance.

After being denied our student visas on September 11, 1991, due to a document omission, on September 20, 1991, all four of us (Michael, Prudence, Carolene, and I) were awarded our shiny new visas with the soaring eagle imprinted in the background. At that defining moment, I felt as though my feet were no longer touching the ground. I could not come to terms with what had just transpired. I had to sit down on a bench in the embassy compound and stay there until I regained consciousness. Not really, but that was how I felt. Moreover, this was the fulfillment of my passionate dream of going to the United States to further my education.

The Final Countdown

Now that all of us had gotten our visas, it was time to press forward because we were up against a very tight schedule. It was crunch time, so I had to make several last-minute

Chapter 10

arrangements. It was one of those happy/sad moments for me, knowing that I was leaving in such an abrupt manner. Aunt Lucy said to me, "Desmond, I don't even have a dollar to give you but just listen to me man, anything is possible when you work hard and put your hope and trust in the Lord. Do you hear mi, man! Just remember to work hard and put your hope and trust in the Lord." Surely, her encouraging words already had paid a big dividend because a total stranger, whom I had never seen, met, or heard of before, had just provided me with a generous gift of $875 U.S. toward my college expenses. Also, my airfare was made available to me free of charge by Mr. Butch Stewart. In fact, Mr. Stewart sponsored all four trainees' airfares. Therefore, at this juncture, I would like to extend my sincere thanks and gratitude to Mr. Butch Stewart for his generosity and sincere act of kindness. Mr. Butch Stewart was the owner and operator of the Sandals all-inclusive resorts and the Appliance Traders Limited Company where I worked for a short period.

Although Aunt Lucy did not possess any financial wealth, I can assure you that she was blessed with a treasure trove of spirituality. Her words meant more to me than all the tangibles of this life. Her comforting words were what kept me going then, and what keeps me going now. The point I am making is this: material things will last for a short time, but hope and trust that is rooted in God will outlast a lifetime.

After all the running around, the drama, and the excitement on the Jamaican side was over, it was Saturday, September 21, 1991, and I was finally getting ready to embark on a whole new journey to boldly go where I had never gone before. Okay, I know my expression sounded a bit Trekkie, but I hope you get the point that I was excited to be embarking on such a life-changing academic journey. Finally, I bid one last goodbye to my sisters, nieces, and nephews.

Before I start cruising at 30,000 feet, I would like to share with you one of my most important discoveries. After having had some time to review my file in the year 2009, I discovered that exactly seven years prior to being awarded this opportunity, I had told my CDA officer, Ms. Davis, that I had dreamt of going to school in the United States of America. Although it was just a dream, Ms. Davis viewed it otherwise and made a note of it in my file. For her to have done that, I had to have told her convincingly. On the one hand, all I had to support my desire was a dream. On the other hand, Ms. Davis most likely had witnessed the yearning desire of a child to succeed and deemed his passion noteworthy.

Back to the day at hand. This opportunity ushered in the dawn of a new era in my life. I will never forget that afternoon when I boarded the American Trans Air flight with $875 in my pocket and a couple of pieces of clothing (not suitable for a Chicago blizzard, of course) stashed away in my suitcase. Despite the financial and other foreseeable limitations, I can assure you that, at that moment, my mind was filled with hope and optimism. As I sat comfortably in my seat and watched the aircraft taxi toward the runway, I could not help but wonder if this experience was real. Within a couple of seconds, the aircraft took off down the runway and before I could get comfortable we were airborne. I found myself staring out the window until I could no longer see the island of Jamaica. And that was

Chapter 10

when it dawned on me that I was really on my way to the United States of America.

It is hard to imagine that it was just like yesterday I found myself living with my father as a Rastafarian; Being forcefully removed from my father's care and transferred to an orphanage where only my basic needs were met, and everything else about the future was considered the unknown; Later being transferred back to my father's care; Only to find myself being transferred from my father's care back to the orphanage; Then from the orphanage to my mother's care where the essentials of life such as food and shelter were not considered the norm; My life was interrupted once more when I was transferred from my mother's care back to the orphanage; Later I was transferred to a foster home where my foster parents' words and actions conveyed a message that my life has no value; Later I was transferred to a temporary foster home; Finally after many years of great upheaval, I was transferred to a wonderful and caring foster mother, Aunt Lucy whose words and actions conveyed a message that I am a person and that my life should be valued. However, on this particular day, I found myself soaring to new heights. It was no longer a dream. Instead, it was now a reality. Although there had been many twists and turns throughout the process, I am grateful that, today, my life is a testament to God's undeserved favor. My life is also a reflection of the wonderful people such as Aunt Lucy and the institutions that have fostered me as I traversed the unknowns. It is in moments like these that I think of my only brother, George, and the fact that he was never allowed to live out his life's dreams.

This was the first time I had left Jamaica and my first time flying on an airplane. I was so overwhelmed by the events that were unfolding before my eyes, I just could not help but express how excited I was to Prudence, one of the other trainees who was sitting beside me. She probably was tired of hearing me expressing my joy but did not want to burst my bubble. This new journey was taking me far away from my family, especially Aunt Lucy, whom I had come to know in such a short time.

Although I was very happy to have received this wonderful opportunity, I can assure you that I was a bit concerned. Mostly because I did not know how all the pieces would come together. However, I was not overly concerned because I remember Aunt Lucy's comforting words, in which she had reminded me on several occasions that with God, all things are possible.

However, before I ventured out on the next phase of life's journey, I would like to take this time, this moment, and this opportunity to express my sincere thanks and gratitude to Ms. Jasmin Wynter for her overwhelming kindness, perseverance, and support. I simply could not have asked anything more of her. She went far above and way beyond her call of duty to assist me in every, and I mean every, way possible.

Thank you very much for choosing to read volume 3 of my autobiography. I hope you have found my Jamaican life experiences informative and, at times, compelling. I hope my tidbit sense of humor brings out your best smiles and even caused you to chuckle a few times as well. If you wish to explore the interesting episodes of my life in the United States of America, please proceed to volume 4 of my autobiography.

JAMAICA - THE JOURNEY

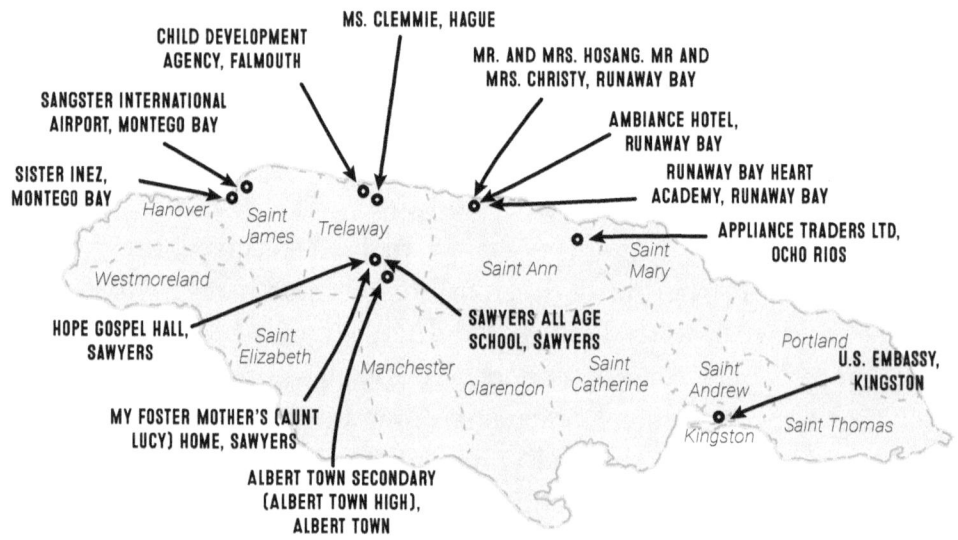

APPENDIX A

THE UNEXPLAINABLE INTERVENTION

I was somewhere between seven and eight years old at the time of this incident I am about to explain. Although at the time, I did not fully understand the magnitude of what really had happened, I did years later when a similar event occurred that made me realize that there has to a God who is always looking out for me. With that said, I would like to share an experience that I would like to describe as The miraculous intervention.

I remember a particular evening when Byron, Bunny, and I were sitting on top of a concrete tank that was being used as a secondary water source for the orphanage. At that time of the evening, we should not have been outside but, instead, in the hall where all the other children were congregated. As we sat there, Bunny and Byron had a discussion regarding who was the better swimmer. Byron told me to jump into the tank and he would come and rescue me. Being naïve, I took off my clothes, opened the little trap door, and jumped into the tank that was filled with water all the way to the very top. That was all I remember until I heard Bunny told me to hold onto the mesh and crawl to where the opening was located. After we both came out of the water, Bunny told me that Byron had gone into the tank but could not find me, so they decided to leave me because they thought that I had drowned. However, he convinced Byron to at least let him take a look before they gave up on trying to save me. With that said, he took off his clothes, jumped into the tank, and searched until he found me.

In retrospect, I can only imagine what was going through their minds at that time. How fearful they must have been, knowing the enormous consequences that awaited them if the unthinkable had happened. As indicated by the picture, I know you may be wondering why it was so challenging to locate a child in a tank of that size. Two factors contributed to why it proved difficult for Byron and Bunny to find me. First, it was a bit dark because it was late in the evening and, second, the bottom of the tank was completely covered with algae and other sludge caused by rotten leaves and trash. In other words, the tank was way overdue for a thorough cleaning. Besides, it was meshed off except for the little access door, and it had greater depth than is revealed by the picture. Back then, the tank was wide open except for the mesh. Today the orphanage has installed a few sheets of zinc to keep out leaves and other debris.

At the time, I did not put much thought into what Byron and Bunny were saying. However, many years later,

The Unexplainable Intervention

I experienced the effects of drowning when I fell into a deep pocket of water while I was navigating the famous Dunn's River Falls. The most frightening aspect was that I found myself fully submerged and immediately started taking in water. Thank God I was quickly rescued by a tourist who was within proximity. It was not until I was writing about my life that the magnitude of what really had happened at the orphanage was revealed unto me. And that was when I realized that the Lord had intervened and saved my life, because I could not have survived being submerged underwater for that period. The outcome of this experience, although unexplainable, it is also undeniable because I did not swallow as much as a teaspoon of water. Based on the scientific evidence, as a result of what Byron and Bunny told me, and the drowning experience I alluded to above, I would definitely not be alive today had the Lord not intervened and saved me.

APPENDIX B

GENEROSITY ABOUNDS

I would like to fill you in on my face-to-face visit with Mr. Franklyn Rance (Frank Rance) some twenty-one years later. This heartfelt moment occurred when I finally had an opportunity to meet him for the very first time on June 20, 2012, and express my thanks and gratitude to him in person. I remember the day I drove up to the security gate of his Franklyn D. Resort hotel, thinking that he would not have the time to speak with me because I did have an appointment. I was surprised when the security guard told me that Mr. Rance could spare me fifteen minutes of his time. Fifteen minutes is only a brief period, especially for me, who is always in need of more time for just about everything. However, in this instance, fifteen minutes was sufficient time for me to express to him how much I appreciated the significant financial contribution he had provided me some twenty-one years earlier. In addition to my "Thank You," I presented him with a short synopsis of my life, and my brother's as well. I also informed him that I was currently writing my autobiography and, in addition to my life's story, I was taking the opportunity to highlight his and the many other acts of kindness that I received as I progressed along life's journey. He suggested that I dedicate

Appendix B

my book to my brother by incorporating the name Woka Man into the title. I have explained the significance of the Woka Man label in volume 4 of my autobiography. After our conversation, I was surprised when I found out that Mr. Rance had spent approximately forty-five minutes of his extremely busy schedule listening to me.

Looking for a family getaway? Look no further than the Franklyn D. Resort (http://www.fdrholidays.com/). I could not resist including a little advert for FDR.

REFERENCES

Reynolds, Ras Dennis Jabari. *Jabari Authentic Jamaican Dictionary of the Jamic Language: Featuring, Jamaican Patwa and Rasta Iyaric, Pronunciations and Definitions.* Around the Way Books, 2006.

Williams, Petre. "'They Beat Us Here.'" *Reformatory Caning in Jamaica, June 2005* – CORPUN ARCHIVE *jmr00506*, Observer Western Bureau, 19 June 2005, http://www.corpun.com/jmr00506.htm.

www.ingramcontent.com/pod-product-compliance
Lightning Source LLC
Chambersburg PA
CBHW021056080526
44587CB00010B/265